WORLDS OF MEMORY AND WISDOM

WORLDS OF MEMORY AND WISDOM

Encounters of Jews and African Christians

**Edited by Jean Halpérin
and Hans Ucko**

Alliance
of independent publishers
for another globalization

The Alliance of Independent Publishers is a non-profit-making association governed by French legislation, set up in Spring 2002 on the initiative of a small group of book professionals. By gradually setting up an international network of publishers, working independently of the major publishing groups, who meet regularly and work together on publishing projects, the Alliance of Independent Publishers is contributing to the circulation of ideas and the building of an international civil society.

The Alliance is committed to promoting solidarity-based commercial agreements between its members, in particular by inspiring and developing co-publishing processes. Linguistic networks (French-speaking, English-speaking, Spanish-speaking, Arabic-speaking, etc.) have been set up for some aspects of our work. Many publishing projects have been initiated, including collections co-published internationally: *Global Issues, Near and Far, Keywords*.

Finally, the Alliance produces dossiers on questions of importance to the publishing profession and promotes the sharing of expertise.

The Alliance of Independent Publishers coordinates these projects, leads the linguistic networks and organises meetings with its members.

The Alliance initiated and coordinated the production of this work, in partnership with World Council of Churches Publications (Switzerland), Editions du Cerf (France), African University Press (Cameroon) and Babel, publishers (Israel); these texts are thus available in English, French and Hebrew.

The publication of this book was made possible by the Harriett and Robert Heilbrunn Institute for International Interreligious Understanding of the American Jewish Committee as well as by the Office on Interreligious Relations and Dialogue of the World Council of Churches, Geneva, Switzerland.

© World Council of Churches Publications, Geneva, 2005
ISBN 2-8254-1429-8

In memory of
Dr. Gerhart Riegner,
initiator of the
African Christian-Jewish dialogue,
and in honour of
Dr. Samuel Kobia,
the first African general secretary
of the World Council of Churches.

Contributors

Denis Charbit, Israel
Professor of Political Science at the Open University of Israel
Author of *Zionisms*; Joint editor of *A universal history of the Jews*

Henri Cohen-Solal, Israel/France
Educator and psychoanalyst
Founding member of Beit Ham, Jerusalem

Jean Halp rin, France
Professor of Jewish Thought at the University of Fribourg
Member, International Jewish Committee on Inter-religious Consultations
Chairman of *Colloque des intellectuels juifs de langue française (Colloquium of French-speaking Jewish intellectuals)*

Andr Karamaga, Rwanda
Currently the Executive Secretary for Africa for the World Council of Churches. He is a former staff member of the All Africa Conference of Churches and a former President of the Presbyterian Church in Rwanda.

Kasonga wa Kasonga, from Congo, is Professor of Theology, with an emphasis on Christian education. He used to head the Christian education and family life programme of the All Africa Conference of Churches (AACC) and is in charge of the programme for theology, mission and evangelism of the same institution.

Hannah Wangeci Kinoti (1941-2001) from Kenya was a pioneering African woman theologian and religious scholar. She obtained a PhD in Religious Studies from the University and worked particularly on the relationship between health and religion. She was an active member of the Circle of Concerned African Women Theologians.

Simon Lauer, Switzerland
Professor of Biblical and Talmudic Studies, University of Lucern
Co-Editor: *Judaica et Christiana*; Co-author: *Die Gleichnisse der Rabbinen (The parables of the Rabbis)*

John Mbiti is an African theologian from Kenya based in Switzerland. He has written extensively on theology, biblical studies, and African religion. Former Director of the Ecumenical Institute Bossey, and retired Professor of the Science of Mission and Extra-European Theology at the University of Bern.

Mmutlanyane Stanley Mogoba is from South Africa. He is a Bishop of the Methodist Church of South Africa and President of the South African political party Pan Africanist Congress of Azania.

Kofi Asare Opoku, a citizen of Ghana, is currently Professor of Religious Studies at Lafayette College, Easton, Pennsylvania, USA.

David Rosen, Israel
Director, Inter-religious Affairs, American Jewish Committee
Former Chief Rabbi of Ireland
Member, International Jewish Committee on Inter-religious Consultations
Past President, International Council of Christians and Jews

Shemaryahu Talmon, Israel
Professor of Bible Studies, Hebrew University of Jerusalem
Author: *King, Cult and Calendar in Ancient Israel; The World of Qumran From Within*

Hans Ucko was born in Sweden and is an ordained minister of the Church of Sweden. He is the Programme Secretary in the Office on Inter-religious Relations and Dialogue of the World Council of Churches, Geneva, Switzerland. He is the editor of the biannual WCC publication *Current Dialogue*.

Walter Wurzburger, USA (1920-2002)
Rabbi, Professor of Ethics, Yeshiva University, New York
Author, Ethics of Responsibility; Co-Editor, Treausry of Tradition

Contents

Preface I

Nothing should ever be taken for granted. This presumably also applies to the African-Jewish encounters that have been taking place now for over fifteen years. Yet, for those who did not have the benefit of participating in these outstandingly successful meetings, this book will allow them to discover a truly novel and fascinating chapter of a genuine intercultural dialogue conducted on an equal footing at the highest level of quality and intellectual integrity.

In this volume, the reader will find no room for commonplaces, complacency, apologetics, hasty generalisations, ill feelings, prejudice, fear, or hidden agendas of any kind.

In their prefaces, Professor Kofi Asare Opoku and Rev. Dr. Hans Ucko assess in detail the scope and impact of the three Consultations which were held successively in Nairobi (1986), Johannesburg (1995) and Yaoundé (2001).

They provided a unique opportunity for Christians coming from Sub-Saharan Africa and for Jews from Europe, North America, Israel and Africa to engage in a fruitful and highly stimulating exchange in the course of which both sides learned a lot about themselves and about the other.

The agenda of each of these meetings had been carefully tailored to the event in consultation with our African partners. We were all aware of the need to avoid topics that could hint at any suspicion of superiority, precedence or domination. Our aim was to focus on subjects pointing to a commonality of concerns and purpose. Hence our will to shape this dialogue in a way rather different from the issues usually raised in similar Jewish-Christian consultations which have been taking place in Europe and America during the last half-century.

In Nairobi, the papers and discussions were devoted to three fundamental subjects:

Ancient wisdom in both cultures and its value for contemporary life; the understanding of Scripture; and Creation in both cultures. Belonging to seemingly totally different backgrounds, we eventually identified close connections and affinities leading to a community of purpose. Such challenging issues as "Revelation", "Monotheism", and "Unity of Humankind" were thus constructively re-visited.

In Johannesburg the debates centred on "Family, Community, and Tradition as a way to the future". These are indeed fundamental questions, common to both cultures: the encounter with the age of modernity; how can we save our traditional family life; how can we sustain our sense of community; how can we maintain and reinforce our religious heritage and our cultural tradition in the face of so many factors of disintegration and dissipation. We discovered that we all shared in different ways the same problems and that we should learn from each other how to control them.

However, due to the fact that the Johannesburg consultation took place shortly after the revolutionary abolition of apartheid, this specific event and the lessons to be drawn from it legitimately ranked high in our thoughts and discussions. We wish to pay tribute to the Jewish personalities who actively participated in the struggle against apartheid.[1]

The third of these Consultations was held in Yaoundé, and the agenda containing the three themes "Shalom and Ubuntu", "Memory and Experiences of Violence" and "The Challenge of Peace-building", was, once again, conceived in a spirit of genuine reciprocity and symmetry.

The papers delivered on "Shalom and Ubuntu" and "Memory and Experiences of Violence" are reproduced in the last part of this volume.

The texts included in this book provide ample food for thought. They will remain of lasting value as a source of inspiration and sound reflection. What they may not have conveyed is the superb comradeship and friendship developed between all participants during these encounters where they shared not only the working sessions but also the meals and times of leisure. This created a wonderful climate of human warmth, which added to the significance of this treble exercise in mutual enlightenment. Each of these encounters was characterized by an atmosphere of freshness, purity, and luminosity, without any biases or constraints, nor any strings attached.

We are happy to share with the readers of this book, which is being published simultaneously in English, French and Hebrew editions, a significant part of the beautiful spiritual crop planted and reaped together on African soil.

Prof. Jean Halpérin   *Rabbi David Rosen*

International Jewish Committee
on Interreligious Consultations

---

[1] Either openly on behalf of Judaism, such as the former chief Rabbis Louis Rabinowitz and Israel Abrahams, or in the awareness that their action was inspired by Jewish values and teachings, such as Helen Suzman, Ellen Hellman, Justice Issy Meisels, Justice Arthur Chaskelson, or Franz Auerbach, to name but a few.

The same values prompted economic and social action led by the Union of Jewish Women as well as the outstanding work done under the auspices of Ikamva Labantu by Helen Lieberman. Add to this in the new South Africa, under the leadership of Nelson Mandela, the impressive initiatives taken by Tikkun, the organization founded by Bertie Lubner with the help of Chief Rabbi Cyril Harris. These groups devote their efforts for the sake of the poor and suffering in South Africa in the spirit of tikkun olam — to improve and heal society.

Preface II

Anyone asked to locate geographically the Jewish-Christian dialogue would most likely put Europe and North America as the venue. Europe offers a history of 2000 years of Christians and Jews living together, North America has become a continent where Jewish identity has established itself and enjoys a spiritual renaissance. There is a particular agenda for Jewish-Christian dialogue in Europe and North America based upon a common history and daily encounters. It is an agenda based upon a demographic situation, where Christians are a majority and Jews a minority. This agenda is not necessarily applicable in a Jewish-Christian dialogue taking place in other parts of the world. Here other issues emerge, other areas are relevant. African Christian-Jewish dialogue is a case in point.

There is an increasing diversity within the Christian community. In a desire to expand the scope of Christian concerns, the World Council of Churches (WCC) has intentionally been seeking a widened spectrum of Christian participation in the Jewish-Christian dialogue. Accentuating the universality and diversity of the church, the WCC wants to facilitate encounters between Jews and Christians from Africa, Asia and Latin America. A productive encounter of theological insights and experiences of Christians and Jews from different parts of the world will prove to be a contribution to both communities. For instance, Jews will discover that Christians by definition are not the majority population in any given country as may be the case in Europe or North America and Christians are not necessarily the ones in power. They will discover Christians in the midst of a theological wrestling with culture, religion, heritage, doctrine and classical theological teaching. Christians, in parts of the world where there is no Jewish community to interact with, will be given the possibility to discover how the Jewish tradition understands the Hebrew Scriptures or Old Testament. And such discoveries may prove to be quite useful in the shaping of new understandings, not only of the Jewish people but also of oneself. African theology seeks to provide more space for Africa in Christian theology and finds inspiration in the Old Testament, which through its images and stories, in more than one way, reflects Africa and her people.

The collection of articles from three different African Christian-Jewish dialogues will demonstrate a diversity of subjects expressing some of the concerns of African Christians. They will indicate how African Christians are in the midst of a creative process making Christianity part of the land and culture and soul of Africa. The following reflections seek to illustrate some aspects of this endeavour and highlight commonalties for the encounter between African Christians and Jews.

The missionary movement of the 18th-19th century began with good intentions but was caught up in the colonial and "civilising" enterprise of the West. The result was an alienating Christianity, which more or less ignored African culture. A Tanzanian Christian pastor once confided in me and said that it had taken him quite some time before he could actually taste the Bread of Life. He said that there was a plastic film wrapped around the Bread of Life all the time. There was no way to penetrate the film and it was difficult to remove. The plastic film was made in the West, solid Western quality and it was wrapped around the Bread of Life, the Gospel. Christianity in Africa like Christianity in Asia with few exceptions is an import from the West and it arrived well covered in Western cultural wrapping; European hymns, European liturgy and European church architecture. There are church buildings in Zimbabwe that are exact replicas of church buildings in the extreme north of Sweden. Missionaries brought that which was dear to them and which they considered as being the only possible expression of what Christian faith was really all about.

African theologians seek to provide space for Africa in Christianity. This movement to contextualise Christian faith in Africa has been going on for decades. In this respect the ecumenical movement has acted as a facilitator, encouraging an exchange of experiences of what it might mean to be a Christian outside the Western framework and to see if it is possible to articulate the Christian story in a way that makes it more at home in Africa.

How can one be true to the heart and soul of Africa while being committed to the tenets of a Christianity which was not born in Africa? African theologian André Karamaga, one of the contributors in this book, said in a meeting of Christian theologians: "The church in Africa lives among Muslims and people following African traditional religions. Within one family, you can have relatives who are deeply committed to Islam or deeply loyal to the ways of African traditional religion. And yet, they all live together in harmony. The church came to Africa from the West. It is a pot-plant: there is a flower and there is a pot, where the flower is supposed to grow. Structure or liturgy makes up the pot. The soil of the pot needs external support for the flower to grow. The pot does not really enable the flower to become truly rooted in the soil of Africa. The pot needs to be broken. But people love the pot as much as they love the flower (the gospel)." This is the dilemma.

Every community needs a culture that is supported by myths, symbols, practices, celebrations, festivals, institutions and liturgical life. In Africa, religion and culture are inextricably bound together and can seldom be discussed apart from each other. Anyone acquainted with Judaism and how it is practised will recognise similar affinities between religion and culture. Religion is the substance of culture, and culture the form of religion. If religions are responses to the Mystery of Life, cultures are expressions of these responses — not only through words and ideas, but also through symbol and sound and colour.

African theology is an attempt to articulate Christian theology by Africans on their own terms within the context of history, culture and contemporary issues. It is about revaluing the thought and culture of traditional Africa, in some ways a theological parallel to the thinking of Léopold Senghor and the principle of "negritude." The All Africa Conference of Churches (AACC) stresses in its various programmes the need for an African theology. Pope Paul VI told Roman Catholic bishops: "you may and you must have an African Christianity" and Catholic theologians in Africa struggle today to keep this vision alive.

African traditional religion, its world-view and values, is a source in African theology. African religion is, says the eminent African theologian John Mbiti, "profoundly monotheistic, resembling the religion of the Jewish (Old) Testament, the proverbs and parables of Jesus". Is the God described in the Bible the same God, who is acknowledged and worshipped in African religion? African theologians say yes, not wanting to limit God to the biblical record.

It is in this context that one also needs to see the African Christian-Jewish dialogue, documented in this book. If one major constituent in the Jewish-Christian dialogue in the West is the theological abuse of Judaism and its consequences in the history of antisemitism, the relationship between African Christians and Jews is played out in a completely different context. Although the export of Western Christianity to Africa also brought theological constructs that built upon polarisations between old and new, law and grace, particularity and universality, etc., African Christians have not put into practice such teachings. African culture and traditional religion resonate with much of the same world-view as the Jewish tradition. A Jewish-Christian dialogue, which in the West to a certain extent must be based upon the correction of prejudice and theological stereotyping and which also to a certain level seems to address Christians more than Jews, has another ground note in Africa. These are first of all the affinities between African religion and the religion of the Old Testament in the understanding of creation, the life cycle and social life. There is a demonstrable predilection for the Old Testament in many expressions of African Christianity and theology. Converts to Christianity seemed less interested in the Old Testament as typology but were more interested in the concrete stories of the Old Testament itself. And it is said that missionaries were actually reluctant to have the Old Testament as the beginning in the instruction of converts, fearing that the atmosphere of the Old Testament would be so close to African culture, religion and life that converts might feel that there was no need to proceed to the New Testament.

The Old Testament offers a paradigm for African theology through the biblical stories about the people of Israel. The importance of rituals, taboos and regulations, dreams, visions and trances as media of the revelation of God are appreciated in the Old Testament, mirroring African culture and religion. Thought-provoking African proverbs, similar to many of the proverbs of the Bible, regard tradition as a guiding principle for the present and the future. The Nairobi consultation opened the door to how the experiences of life are expressed through sayings, proverbs and adages.

In addition, Jews and Africans have experienced a similar history, a history of the denigrated, of having memories and experiences of exclusion, exploitation and violence, i.e. antisemitism, the Shoah, slave trade, apartheid and the genocide in Rwanda. The consultations in Johannesburg and Yaoundé witnessed to how Christians and Jews wrestled with the memories and experiences of denigration, death and destruction.

It is of course a truism to say that Africa and Africans belong together. But the Jewish history has also its particular relationship to Africa. There is a Jewish and African encounter in ancient Egypt. Various interested parties discuss whether the ancient Egyptians were Semites, of Mediterranean origin, or came from Africa. Reference to the Edfu Text, found in the Temple of Horus at Edfu, is often made as to the early history of the Nile Valley. This document states among other things that civilisation was brought from the south by a band of invaders under the leadership of King Horus. It is said that black Africans from Kes, to the south, took over Egypt, bringing a "renaissance" of art, religion and culture, and a resurgence of military power. African empires of cultural, religious and political achievement existed and sometimes seem to have taken hold in and over Egypt, something that runs contrary to scholars who claim that no significant civilisation ever existed in Africa. We know from graves in Egypt that there were people of African stock and yet, beyond assigning to Africans the role of being servants, Egyptology rarely acknowledges ancient Egypt's African heritage or cultural roots.

Egypt was not always black African, as Afrocentrists would have it. There are archaeologists who claim that a Semitic people penetrated predynastic Egypt. We know that the language contained a strong Semitic element. The Hebrew Bible refers to Ham, the son of Noah, as one way of explaining the relationship with Africa (Gen. 10,6), although the story about Ham is disparaging and was early turned into a comfortable argument both for racism and slavery in all three monotheistic religions.

The Hebrew Bible makes recurrent references to Africa, Cush. The river Gihon, one of the rivers in the Garden of Eden, "is the one that flows around the whole land of Cush" (Gen. 2,13). The apocryphal Book of Jubilees (135-105 BCE) presents us with the earliest attempt to identify the river Gihon as the river Nile. The account of restored families of the earth after the Flood incorporates Africa (Gen. 10). The bondage and exodus from Egypt took place in Africa. In various cultures, we are familiar with King Solomon's relation with the Queen of Sheba, who had come to visit him. Upon returning home, she gave birth to a son, whom she named Ibn al-Hakim, "son of the wise man" according to Arab tradition. Some Jewish, Islamic and Persian sources state that this child was Nebuchadnezzar. Ethiopians believe him to be David II (the name given him by Solomon), who later called himself Menelek, and who was the first king of the Ethiopian dynasty.

Psalm 87 extols Africa as having its rightful home in Zion. "On the holy mount stands the city he founded; the LORD loves the gates of Zion more than all the dwellings of Jacob. Glorious things are spoken of you, O city of God. Selah. Among those who know me I mention Rahab and Babylon; Philistia too, and Tyre, with Ethiopia — This one was born there, they say." Africa is thus at the centre of Zion. Africa is in the very heart of Jerusalem.

A leap into our times demonstrates yet another link between the Jewish people and Africa, which seen with contemporary eyes, of course has all the trappings of a colonialist mindset. Theodor Herzl, in his dream for a Jewish homeland, entered into negotiations with the British government, which offered him Uganda, the territory, which was then British East Africa, below Egypt and Ethiopia. Herzl brought the offer to the Sixth Zionist Congress in 1903. The Zionist movement was nearly torn apart in the ensuing battle between those willing to accept this offer of land in Africa and those who saw return to Palestine as the only option. It is doubtful whether anyone bothered to ask Africans themselves what they thought about the prospect of a having a Jewish national home in Uganda.

In various aspects and at various times in history Jews and Africans have intersected. There are relations and associations between the narratives and histories of Jews and Africans. One needs to be grateful to the Central Committee of the WCC in August 1992 calling for a Jewish-Christian dialogue that went beyond the traditional actors in this encounter. The Central Committee, aware of the growing plurality of the Christian community, encouraged Christians also from countries where there were no Jewish communities to take part in the Jewish-Christian dialogue. All issues of substance, which arise in any segments of the Jewish and Christian communities, should be worthy of exploration, not only those which are on the agenda for official consultations between Jews and Christians. This wish was greatly rewarded in Nairobi, Johannesburg and Yaoundé, something that is recorded with emphasis in this book.

A Jewish-Christian dialogue, involving encounters between African or Asian Christians and Jews will leave the North Atlantic rim, which has been the classical venue for Jewish-Christian dialogue so far. Such encounters open new avenues in Jewish-Christian relations, which in the end will contribute to a renewal of the Jewish-Christian dialogue itself. New themes and partners are involved. The diversity in the Jewish tradition and the various interpretations of Old Testament texts seem to inspire a re-reading of the Old Testament among Christians in Africa and Asia. This could enable another view, one that does not only serve as a typology for the New Testament but offers new and relevant hermeneutics, contributing to the development of contextual theologies. They could further provide new nuances in the old debate on the role of the Old Testament in Christian theology. Jews, on the other hand, in the encounter with African Christians may discover the plurality of Christianity and realise that Christians today are much more than traditional Christendom and that the centre of Christianity now is rather in the South than in the North or in the West.

The contributions from the encounters and consultations in Nairobi 1986, Johannesburg 1995 and Yaoundé 2001 bear witness to the opening up of new chapters in the Jewish-Christian dialogue, enriching both Jews and Christians. In this way, these consultations substantiate the "Focus on Africa", which the WCC Assembly in Harare ushered in in 1998, calling on the ecumenical family to accompany the churches in Africa on a journey towards a new vision for Africa. But this focus has not only a new vision for Africa but enables also a vision coming out of Africa. The learnings coming out of the African Christian - Jewish consultations demonstrate the life-affirming strength of Africa, a vibrant continent of resilience in spite of hardships. The African Christian-Jewish dialogue in Yaoundé provided something of this spirit, not only intellectual exchanges around a table, but a sharing in each other's worship life, prayer and celebration in the presence of the other. Enriched by such fellowship, this consultation managed to approach in depth sensitive questions about suffering, about violence and how to right the wrongs and not succumb to yet more violence.

The African Christian-Jewish dialogues have opened new perspectives not only to the protagonists themselves but also to the oikoumene at large and people of all faiths. These dialogues address questions relevant to a life of human dignity and hope. The WCC, in recognition of what these dialogues have meant for those participating and others interested in the issues, can only express gratitude for the possibility of working together with Dr. Gerhard Riegner of blessed memory and Professor Jean Halpérin. Both insisted on the necessity of Jewish-Christian dialogue, both of them eager and always willing to open new doors for dialogue beyond and between cultures and continents.

Hans Ucko
Office on Interreligious Relations and Dialogue
World Council of Churches

Introduction

The idea to hold an African Christian-Jewish Consultation was hatched in November 1984 during a chance encounter between the late Dr. Gerhart Riegner and this writer at a Consultation on Religious Pluralism, jointly sponsored by the World Council of Churches and the International Jewish Committee on Interreligious Consultations at Harvard University. Dr. Riegner and I had dinner at a Jewish Synagogue in Cambridge, Massachusetts, and it was in the course of our stimulating conversation that the possibility of such an event was discussed. It became clear to me, then, that both of us had been thinking along the same lines and were only looking for a partner to move the idea forward.

My involvement in the programmes of the World Council of Churches during the early 70s had brought me to what I considered a limitation in the course and content of the dialogues taking place between European Christians and Jews. I found that these dialogue encounters were overburdened by feelings of guilt, the result of centuries of European persecution of the Jewish people, from the Middle Ages to the twentieth century, culminating in the Shoah. It seemed to me that these feelings of guilt on the part of European Christians were then through the Jewish-Christian dialogue generously shared with *all* Christians.

When thinking about encounters between African Christians and Jews, I felt that we as Christians from Africa would have something of our own to offer the Jewish-Christian dialogue, something which could point the way to fruitful and mutually rewarding dialogues. In such dialogues with non-European Christian partners, the hope was also entertained that the European stranglehold on Biblical interpretation would be lessened, and the opportunity for other equally valid and broader interpretations of Scripture would arise, leading to greater understanding of Scripture. This hope was based on the African proverb: *"Truth (knowledge or wisdom), is like a baobab tree, and one person's arms cannot embrace it."* The European interpretation was certainly one arm attempting to embrace the baobab tree of Biblical interpretation, but other arms joined together would bring us all to a fuller and more complete understanding.

The basis of my confident expectation of the immense value of an African Christian-Jewish consultation lay in the fact that African traditional culture and ancient Hebraic traditions share an affinity with each other, and even though contemporary Jews and their African counterparts no longer live like their ancestors, both are successors to venerable and cherished traditions that continue to shape their responses to modernity. Besides, the felicitous and poignant appeal of the Hebrew

Scriptures to African Christians, many of whom came to accept Christianity because of their predilection for the Hebrew Scriptures, whose worldview is very close to that of Africa, provided an enduring and profitable basis for dialogue. Furthermore, the absence of barriers of any kind between the two groups, who are living examples of the inimitable triumph of the human spirit over centuries of relentless persecution, oppression and even genocide, made dialogue between them an intriguing possibility with far-reaching implications, not only for harmonious relations between Christians and Jews, generally, but also for peace on our planet.

Dr. Riegner, for his part, had had a long-nursed interest in, and abiding concern for, broadening the scope of Christian-Jewish dialogue by creating opportunities for African Christians and Jewish people to dialogue with each other. The breadth of Dr. Riegner's vision of the world and his transparent and sterling sincerity were borne out by his untiring efforts and the judicious and consummate leadership he provided in the effort to bring about an African Christian-Jewish Consultation.

The Nairobi Consultation

The first African Christian-Jewish Consultation, sponsored by the World Council of Churches, the International Jewish Committee on Interreligious Consultations and the All-Africa Conference of Churches, was held in Nairobi, Kenya, from November 10-13, 1986. The Consultation brought together twelve Jewish scholars from North America, Europe and Israel and ten Africans from six African countries — Ethiopia, Ghana, Kenya, Nigeria, Sierra Leone and Tanzania, representing both Protestant and Orthodox traditions and made up of theologians, clergymen and lay people.

This was the first time that African Christians and Jewish people had met at such a high level of mutual consultation and the papers spanned a whole range of concerns, from "Biblical Wisdom in Rabbinic Garb" to "Ancient Wisdom in the African Heritage" and from "Creation in African Religion" to "The Biblical Understanding of Creation and the Human Commitment". Significantly, the meeting was on African soil and the agenda was African, not European. The discussions were firmly grounded in a commonality of shared concern of Jews and Africans with tradition and its relationship to Scripture. The encounter brought about a crucial realization that had either been overlooked or not fully appreciated in the past, that sustained and relevant Jewish-Christian dialogue was not restricted to areas where Jewish people live with non-Jews, as in the case in Europe, for example, but that Jewish-Christian dialogue could take place in situations and geographical areas even where there are few Jews or none at all.

At Nairobi, the participants faced each other without historical barriers, a fact that brought a new dimension, even freshness, to dialogue. Right from the beginning of our four-day consultation, there was a visibly pervasive and irrepressible anticipation that through our mutual discussions and frank interactions, we would come to understand ourselves better and learn from each other. We also hoped that the results of our mutual interactions would bear worthy fruit and set into motion mutually beneficial relations between Christians and Jews, by going beyond the mere exchange of words into concrete and lasting sharing. Lasting friendships were begun at Nairobi, and Dr. Riegner's statement, "This was the first but it won't be the last such encounter", amply expressed the unanimous sentiment felt by all participants that this experience must be continued.

The Johannesburg Consultation

The second African-Christian Jewish Consultation, again sponsored by the World Council of Churches and the International Jewish Committee on Interreligious Consultations, was held in Johannesburg, South Africa, in June 1995, with the theme, Family, Community and Tradition. This Consultation turned out to be one of the first international gatherings to take place in South Africa after the collapse of apartheid. African participants from Botswana, Cameroon, Eritrea, Ghana, Kenya, Mozambique, Nigeria and South Africa met with their Jewish counterparts from Israel, South Africa, Zimbabwe, Europe and USA.

The discussions at the Consultation centred on themes that are crucial to both Africans and Jews, facing the modern and increasingly technology-driven world, with its attendant pressures and challenges to families, communities and traditions. Scholarly papers on the theme as well as on the effects of apartheid on the African family were followed by penetrating discussions that led to mutual sharing of ideas from both groups of participants.

The publication of the proceedings of the Johannesburg Consultation in the "Trinity Journal of Church and Theology" (vol. VIII 9/1998), published by the Trinity College in Ghana, was an event of great significance, since it was the first time that the proceedings of a Jewish-Christian dialogue had been published in an African theological journal.

An event of immense significance during the Johannesburg Consultation was the visit of the participants to the Hector Pieterson Memorial in Soweto. Hector, a young thirteen-year-old boy, and several of his fellow school children, were gunned down by the apartheid police for holding a protest march against the apartheid government's ruling that made Afrikaans, the language of the Dutch descendants in South Africa, the medium of instruction in secondary schools. The killing of the unarmed school children added to the untold suffering of Africans in apartheid South Africa and recalled many such previous tragedies.

The participants in the Consultation in a singular act of solidarity with the African people in their stout-hearted struggles and bitter experiences of slavery, colonialism, oppression, exploitation and genocide, gathered in Soweto to read Psalms, pray and meditate, not in front of a

11

memorial to Jewish victims, but to Africans — school children, men and women. The participants made the eloquent and weighty point that human suffering is the urgent and paramount concern of all humans and that, as the Akan proverb puts it: *Nnipa nyinaaa ye Onyame mma; obi nye asase ba* — all human beings are the children of God; none is a child of the earth. This event was a refreshing departure from such occasions in previous Jewish-Christian dialogues. As Hans Ucko expresses it: "In some way therefore the memorial in Soweto personifies the plight of the whole of Africa and the reading of Scripture and prayer became that day a common celebration of acquired freedom for the people of South Africa and an expression of solidarity with all the peoples of Africa".

The Yaound Consultation

The third African Christian-Jewish Consultation was held at the Protestant Theological Faculty in Yaoundé, Cameroon, November 8-13, 2001, and it was the first Christian-Jewish dialogue in Francophone Africa, and as many of the African participants aptly expressed it, "the World Council of Churches finally took notice of French-speaking Africa." The Consultation centred its discussions on three themes that were of immediate concern to Jews and Africans: "Shalom and Ubuntu", "Memory and Experience of Violence" and "Challenges to Peace-Building."

The Consultation brought together twenty-five participants. The Jewish participants came from France, Israel, Switzerland and the USA and the African contingent was made up of participants, both clergy and lay people, from Benin, Burundi, Cameroon, Congo Brazzaville, Côte d'Ivoire, Democratic Republic of the Congo, Kenya, Rwanda, South Africa and Togo. Among the African participants were representatives from two of the largest African-founded churches, the Harrist Church and the Kimbanguist Church, and this fact represented a refreshing inclusiveness that opened doors for the expression of a wider range of interpretations of Scripture.

Beyond the mutually enriching intellectual exchanges, participants also shared insights into the interpretation of Scripture in joint Bible studies. Furthermore, the sharing of the participants in each other's worship life, Jewish and Christian, turned out to be an uplifting spiritual experience for all. As one Jewish participant put it: "I entered the church with some reservation, but never before has participating in a Christian worship been so meaningful". Certainly, the African approach to worship was a significant factor in this reaction and is indeed a remarkable contribution to Christian-Jewish dialogue.

The distance from the Jewish Synagogue in Cambridge, Massachusetts to Nairobi, Kenya, to Johannesburg and its nearby township of Soweto and to Yaoundé, Cameroon is indeed a long one, but between the landmarks, many propitious events of lasting significance had taken place.

Contrary to the assumption that Christians who live in parts of the world where there is an insignificant Jewish presence or history are not immediately part of Jewish-Christian dialogue, the outcome of the three Consultations so far has shown how wide off the mark the old assumption was. Any Christian who reads the Bible is in dialogue with Judaism, whether or not he or she realizes it and therefore African Christians dialoguing with Jews is nothing out of the ordinary. Besides, the tremendous growth of Christianity in Africa, especially in the twentieth century, has made the continent one of the contemporary centres of Christianity, and the interpretation of Scripture by Africans and its contribution to Christian theology in general, must be welcomed as insights providing enriching contributions. Our African ancestors said, *However big one eye may be, two are better.*

At the Yaoundé Consultation, participants wrestled with the issues of punitive justice and retributive justice. The Holocaust was followed by the Nuremberg Trials (retributive justice), and Apartheid was followed by the Truth and Reconciliation Commission (restorative justice). Both forms of justice grew out of age-old traditions that have informed jurisprudence in different societies, and the participants had the opportunity to reflect on the challenge that the African notion of ubuntu and restorative justice presents to the world community. This urgent and relevant issue lies beyond the narrow confines of what has passed for Jewish-Christian dialogue in the past and this opportunity arose only because the occasion was a meeting between Jews and African Christians, but the implications are of world-wide interest in the global efforts at bringing a just society into being.

The concerns of Jewish-Christian dialogue must begin to be seen in their wider context as human concerns in which all of us have interest and a contribution to make. Our African ancestors said, *Hunt in every forest, for there is wisdom and good hunting in all of them,* to express their recognition of the truth that every geographical location has it own unique hunting opportunities and has something beneficial to offer. Whether the dialogue encounter is between Jews and Africans or Asians, something good is bound to accrue to the benefit of all humankind and it is this awareness that makes the Consultations between African Christians and Jews welcome and propitious events that could lead to the promotion of friendship, peace and mutual understanding.

This volume serves as an historical record of the African Christian-Jewish Consultations held in three African countries between 1986 and 2001. It is our fervent hope that the papers included here will not only preserve the buoyant spirit of these important discussions but that they will inspire future generations to continue the fruitful interchange between Jewish people and Christians begun in Africa by extending it to other parts of the globe, fostering harmonious relations based on greater mutual understanding. For, it is our conviction that the animosities of the past and even the present, which make dialogue among the peoples of the world an urgent necessity, are not an eternal order cast in granite, but an historical experience whose intensity can be considerably abated when people face each other and dialogue. As the Akan adage puts it, *Conflicts are resolved best with the tongue and not with an axe.*

Kofi Asare Opoku

Nairobi 1986

Biblical wisdom in Rabbinic garb

English-speaking and Sanskrit-speaking people are related to one another. Those who partake in the Hebrew and, in a way, as I believe, also in Greek scripture are related in a sort of 'theology of philology'. This is in no way disparaged by the fact that no English-speaker would understand a word of Sanskrit without painstaking study of that language. Much less is it disparaged by the fact that our modern languages are no longer the same as those of our forebears — few Germans would understand Luther's Bible translation. Although the distance between biblical Hebrew and Tannaitic or Amoraic Palestinian Hebrew is much smaller than that between, for example, twentieth century German and sixteenth century German, the distance is there and it is clearly perceived by every student of the subject. The very fact of this distance may be deplored by some Saddu-ceans. For rabbinic Judaism, it is not only a consequence of the really deplorable and deplored fate of the second Jewish Commonwealth; it also has an advantage: the linguistical shift opens up new vistas on the scriptures, so that we can now see what, in earlier times, was — perhaps providentially — hidden from our eyes. This means that rabbinic reading of the Bible can be done with very good conscience, even though rabbinic explanation rarely holds the water of modern scholarly exegesis.

There is one more aspect of rabbinic explanation. It is meant to teach people how to live while abiding with the Torah. This teaching may take the form of legal rules or formulae or else of literary forms like popular etymologies, moving single words about as if the Bible were a chess board, anecdotes, fables, stories and parables. The rabbis have an explanation for this double-faced exegesis — these two faces being often combined. They say, "When people had change in their pockets, they liked listening to a word of Mishnah or Talmud. But nowadays you would hardly find a penny, and moreover we are sick from the oppression; so people would rather like to hear a word from the Bible and Haggadah." [1]

The texts which I am going to present here originated in a situation which may be described as follows. The Jewish settlement in Judaea dwindled and lost its impact completely. Jews moved to Lower Galilee and were now exposed to the linguistic influences of Aramaic and — especially — Greek. They were allowed a more or less small degree of self-government, but always under the rule of the Imperium Romanum and its usually unscrupulous representatives. People no longer spoke biblical Hebrew. They were rather poor so they especially liked listening to the Bible or the Haggadah. The social status of this audience is reflected in two ways: (a) there are a lot of foreign words in haggadic texts. This would seem to be a mark of popular speech rather than of a claim to sophistication on the part of the speakers, as I. Low suggests. (I once learned that "spectacles" was more popular English than "glasses"; I could quote similar phenomena in French or German.) (b) It is understandable that people who dream of "the good life" (which they know full well that they cannot possibly attain), are fascinated by the most fanciful reports from a royal palace. Therefore, kings, queens and princes are very frequently referred to.

Now what has all this to do with wisdom? The twofold purpose of rabbinic literature in general is to achieve at least fear of God, that is respect, not anxiety, and — as the very ideal — love of God. This purpose is served by the legal interpretation of the Torah which, however, must necessarily be completed by a non-legalistic, edifying formulation of what makes a humane person. Let me stress the fact that these two literary genres are not necessarily distinguished from one another, as man and woman are complementary but different beings; it is not only the same man who expresses these views, but he also may well voice them in one and the same dictum. In short, rabbinic wisdom means teaching people the right way to live as a member of a chosen and persecuted people: to believe in God and his rule; to look at other people in order to follow the lead of the good; and to part company with the wicked.

The texts which I have chosen to illustrate rabbinic wisdom are taken from a midrashic collection which was completed early in the sixth century in Palestine and which contains much older material, too. It is a collection of homilies on single verses of the portions of the Torah, as read on special occasions in the synagogue. The artistic device is to combine a verse mostly from the Hagiographa with a verse from the Pentateuch. The parables contained in these homilies (their number is 133) appeared only a few months ago in a German translation, with extensive commentaries and a lengthy introduction.[2] Professor Clemens Thoma and I carried out this work during five years of the closest imaginable cooperation — in itself proof that ecumenical work in depth *is* possible. Indeed, Professor Thoma and I are united in the firm credo that proper and sober scholarly work, done by persons deeply rooted in their respective faiths, is absolutely necessary, the condition *sine qua non*, of every interreligious dialogue, if the latter is not meant to result in delusion — *nemini bono*.

By way of introduction, a few words must be said about the structure of most of the parables to be quoted in this paper. First, there has to be some motivation for telling a parable. In the case of Pesiqta deRav Kahana, it is more often than not the particular liturgy of the day which calls for a new expression of wisdom — in rabbinic parlance: a *hiddush* or (in modern linguistic terminology) a disclosure. The body of a rabbinic parable consists of a profane account (mashat) for a sacred text *(nimshal)*'; there must, of course, be some analogies between the text and its account. (The lay-out of the first and the third parables in this paper is intended to make these analogies clearly perceptible; in our book, we have applied this method throughout.) Finally, a parable has its addressees according to whom the *hiddush* must be appropriated.[3]

1. The history of God with his people starts with the Exodus in the larger sense, i.e. including all the events connected with it. Of course, the country where most of these events occurred has been characterized in different ways from biblical times on. One of these characterizations is found in Deuteronomy 4:20: "But the Lord hath taken you and brought you forth out of the iron furnace, even out of Egypt, to be unto him a people of inheritance, as ye are are this day." The expression "furnace of iron" also occurs in 1 Kings 8:51. Now, we read in a later addition to the Pesiqta deRav Kahana:

> Rabbi Simeon ben Eleazar said: With what may the Inclination to evil *[yezer ha-ra* — evil inclination] be compared?
>
> With iron put into fire.   It is the same with the Inclination to evil

So long as the iron is in the fire, one may make of it any implement one pleases	The words of the Tora are the only means of coping with it, as it is said: "Is not my word like as a fire? saith the Lord" (Jeremiah 23:29).[4]

In order to appreciate the wisdom-component of this parable, we have to quote its context: the history of Israel's development from a people of slaves to a people of free persons is — at least implicitly — compared with the growing up of man. As it is said in Genesis 8:21, "for the imagination of man's heart is evil from his youth". According to the rabbis,[5] this means that the inclination to good is born, as it were, only later in life. Until then — i.e. until the age of 13 years and 1 day in the case of a male person, or 12 years and 1 day in the case of a female — the working of the inclination to evil really creates problems — as everybody knows. Rabbi Simeon ben Eleazar tells his audience how to deal with these problems. It is no use suppressing the inclination to evil or trying to eliminate it altogether because this inclination is part and parcel of man as created by God. Rather have we to deal with it as we do with iron in the fire, i.e. by making something good out of evil by means of the Torah. By "Torah" we should understand not only the canonical books of the Bible, but also the rabbinic interpretation; because, immediately after this parable, the Pesiqta quotes the school of Rabbi Ismael, saying "My son, if this ugly person comes across you, drag him into the house of study!"

2. The Exodus-story is also a Pharaoh-story; no wonder, then, that Pharaoh's personality is discussed in rabbinic literature. A parable applies to him what is said in Proverbs 17:10: "a reproof entereth more into a wise man than an hundred stripes into a fool." In order to render this verse fit for use in the parable, the darsan applies the hermeneutical device (BBB 119 B) "Rearrange the verse and explain it (*saris qera we-dorsehu)* So we have to concentrate on three words — according to

the repeated hardening of Pharaoh's heart, namely: stripes, fool, a hundred. The parable reads as follows:

> Rabbi Ismael taught: The hundred stripes for a fool may be understood by the parable of a king who said to his servant: "Go get me a fish from the market." The servant went and brought him a fish which stank. The king said, "As you live, you will not escape one of three punishments: You will eat the stinking fish, or you will receive a hundred stripes, or you will pay a fine." The servant said: "I will eat the stinking fish." But no sooner had he begun to eat the stinking flesh than it nauseated him, and he said: "I would rather receive stripes." He had absorbed no more than fifty stripes when he said, "I will pay the fine." Thus he ate stinking flesh, *and* got stripes, *and* paid a fine.

> So, too, the Holy One said to the wicked Pharaoh: "As you live, you will receive ten stripes, or you will pay a fine out of your wealth, or you will let Israel go." You will receive ten stripes — the ten plagues; you will pay a fine out of your wealth — "And they spoiled the Egyptians" (Exodus 12:36); and you will let Israel go — "And it came to pass, when Pharaoh had let the people go" (Exodus 13:17).[6]

From a formal point of view, this parable would not seem to have its right place here. For, when considering the correspondence of *mashal* and *nimsal*, i.e. the "worldly"-human story on the one side and the biblical story behind the "worldly" one, you see that the motif of eating stinking fish is not taken up — I do not know of any instance of such disgraceful doing in the Bible — and, second, that there is no "worldly" counterpart to the dismissal of the Israelites by Pharaoh. Apparently, we have here a kind of pattern: to flee from one evil, only to find another. This can be compared with Amos 5:19: "As if a man did flee from a lion, and a bear met him". Or there is a choice between three things — three punishments in our case — as, for example, in 1 Chronicles 21:10-14, where, however, King David makes an *intelligent* choice; the possibility of a *foolish* choice is illustrated by our parable. In accordance with the fact that the motives do not square fully, one has to describe the contents of this parable as follows: to receive one hundred stripes means to suffer the ten plagues; to pay a fine means to be despoiled by the Israelites; not to be able to endure all the punishments means to be forced to let the Israelites go. Now, it would seem to me that a teaching like "When making a choice, don't be a fool" would belong to a fairly common-place sort of "wisdom", unless we keep in mind that the parable is told about Pharaoh. That may suggest that there is a sort of inner dynamics in stubbornness and foolishness, and man has to be very careful not to be caught in it.

3. We now come to a much later period in Jewish history. Israel is in its own land, well-established. But now God has very tangible claims: Jews have to pay tithes — to this very day, and even outside the Holy Land. Of course, most people never liked paying taxes. On the last day of each of the pilgrimage festivals, we read the portion of the Torah beginning with Deuteronomy 14:22: "Thou shalt truly tithe all the

increase of thy seed, that the field bringeth forth year by year". But Job says: "If my land cry against me, or that the furrows likewise thereof complain" (Job 31:38). The verse intimates that God was asking Job, "Will you own more than three cubits of the earth when you die? How, then, do you presume to say 'If my land cry against me' as though the earth were all yours?" And now follow twin-parables. The first is:

The elder Rabbi Hiyya explained God's question to Job by the story of a man selling a cloak in the market. Someone passed by, saw the cloak, and said "It is mine".

The man selling the cloak replied:	Likewise the Holy One said to Job: Am I not the One of whom it is written:
"Wrap yourself in it. If it fits you, it is yours.	"Do not I fill heaven and earth?" (Jeremiah 23:24)
Otherwise, it is not yours!"	And yet you say: "If against me my earth cry out" (Job 31:38) — as though the earth were your property.

The second parable:

Rabbi Simeon ben Halafta explained God's question to Job by the story of a man selling a maidservant in a market. Someone passed by, saw her, and said "She is mine." the man selling her replied: "Look commandingly at her. If she trembles, she is yours." Likewise the Holy One said to Job: "Am I not the One of whom it is written: 'Who looks on the earth, and it trembleth; He toucheth the mountains, and they smoke' (Psalms 104:32)." "If she does not tremble, she is not yours." "And yet you say 'If against me my earth cry out' — as though the earth were your property." [7]

The salesman means God; "someone" is Job, or any member of the Jewish community who may have problems with tithing. The cloak and the slave are earthly goods which cannot just be vindicated without ado; one has to prove one's ownership. The *mashal* seems to be misleading, in a way, because one might think that the quarrel between seller and buyer remains open. It is the *nimsal* which renders the overall judgement: God is the only proprietor of all the land; when man is dead he is allotted just the space to contain his corpse. Therefore, one is obliged to tithe in order "that thou mayest learn to fear the Lord thy God always" (Deuteronomy 14:23). Thus, this parable is an exposition of a verse and at the same time it is actualizing it. These are two of the different functions a parable can have.

In order to finish with a sort of a climax, I should like to revert to the first example, namely the ways of coping with the "Inclination to evil".[8]

Rabbi Juda the Prince said: "With whom may the Inclination to evil be compared? With a brigand. When he was captured, he was asked, 'Who were your mates?' and he replied, 'So-and so, and So-and-so', saying to himself, 'Since I am to be executed, let them also be executed with me.' Therefore he who heeds the Inclination to evil will fall into Gehenna; because it is said: 'The eyes of the wicked fail' (Job 11:20)."

This parable also has a twin; this illustrates the sentence which serves as a joint to both parables: "The wicked — repentance is open to them, yet they do not turn towards repentance."

A parable of a band of renegades who rebelled against their king: When the king seized them and shut them up in prison, what did they do? They made an opening in the prison wall and got away, except for one who did not flee. In the morning, when the king found him, the king said: "Fool, the opening was before you, and yet you did not free yourself. Your companions who have freed themselves, how can I possibly punish them?" Likewise, the Holy One says to the wicked who fail to see that they can free themselves: "They lose the chance to flee" (Job 11:20). As for the righteous who do not heed the Inclination to evil, the fire of Gehenna cannot have dominion over them.

Incidentally, this parable also refers to Qpheleth 4:13, 14: "Better is a poor and wise child than an old and foolish king, who will no more be admonished. For out of prison he cometh to reign."

Although it appears from a comparison of the text in the Pesiqta deRav Kahana with the version in other midrashic collections that the second parable has been altered somewhat in order to fit in with the first parable, we may well consider them both together. In this way we can also have a look at a crucial problem of parable-interpretation in general.

The two parables both have a "pivot" and a "point". In the first parable the pivot is found where the captured brigand drags his two mates into the prison, the point being that now all of them are hanged. This sort of death-sentence for all the culprits would appear to be typical for man only. In the second parable, where the king (i.e. God) also has a part to play, the resulting point is that only one of the renegades meets his fate, whereas his two fellows who — in a pivot featuring the exact inversion of the first one — are allowed, nay encouraged, to escape from prison. This clearly is the opposite of current human thinking — rightly so, *sub specie Dei misericordis.*

Let me add that we are no longer so sure that the second parable may be compared with Luke 16:19-31. The application of our study of rabbinic parables to New Testament exegesis is so formidable a task that it has to be left to the specialist. I am lucky to tell you that an extremely able scholar, Peter Dschulnigg DD, is already at work.

Biblical wisdom cannot be imitated; the rabbis of old had to adapt its teachings to the comprehension of their contemporaries, as, indeed, every generation of teachers has to do. This rabbinic variety of wisdom may deal with fairly commonplace problems, but it very often tends to endow every-day life with a loftier meaning; just think of a man wrapped in a cloak which may fit him very well, but never so well as heaven and earth fit their maker. Let us look for the immortal meaning of perishable things, so that we may be able to live by them.

Simon Lauer

NOTES

[1] *Shir Kabbah,* 2:5, Vilna edition (reprinted Jerusalem 1975), II, 29b; cf. *Pesiqta deRav Kahana,* 12:3, edited by B. Mandelbaum (New York 1962), I, 205.

[2] Clemens Thoma and Simon Lauer, *Die Gleichnisse der Rabbinen: Pesiqta deRav Kahana* (The Parables of the Rabbis: Pesiqta deRav Kahana) (Berne 1986).

[3] All the parables quoted are from the very good and valuable translation by W. G. Braude and I. J. Kapstein, *Pesikta de Rab Kahana* (London 1975).

[4] *Pesiqta deRav Kahana,* appendix 3, ed. Mandelbaum, II, 461; Thoma and Lauer, 324f.

[5] *Qphelet Rabbah,* 4:15, Vilna edition (reprinted Jerusalem 1975), II, 119a.

[6] *Pesiqta deRav Kahana,* 11:3, ed. Mandelaum, I,' 178f.; Thoma and Lauer, 173-5.

[7] *Pesiqta deRav Kahana,* 10:7, ed. Mandelbaum, I, 168; Thoma and Lauer, 170-2.

[8] *Pesiqta deRav Kahana,* appendix 3, ed. Mandelbaum, II, 461; Thoma and Lauer, 326-9.

Ancient wisdom in the African heritage

Let me begin with an Akan folk-tale from Ghana which explains how wisdom spread to all parts of the world. Once, Ananse the spider, who is the hero of most Akan folk-tales, swept up all wisdom, gathered it together in one spot and placed it in a big gourd and decided to hang it on a very tall tree so that all wisdom on earth would be finished. Ananse took the gourd to the tree which he thought would serve his purpose, and stopped. He took a string and tied it to the gourd, and hung it in front of him. After pausing for while to steady the gourd, Ananse began to climb the tree. But with the gourd in front of him it was very difficult for him to get a good grip on the tree trunk. He tried several times to climb the tree but could not and so he paused to think.

Ananse did not think that any of the members of his household had seen what he was up to, but he was mistaken. His son, Ntikuma, had followed his father, curious to see just what Ananse was going to do. And as Ananse scratched his head in search of a solution to his problem, he was startled by a loud laugh behind him and he turned to find, to his utter amazement, his son, Ntikuma, who, standing a good distance away and gazing intently at his father, suggested to him that if he would put the gourd on his back instead of on his belly he would find it easier to climb the tree.

Ananse was furious, for while he thought that he had collected all wisdom in one place, yet some remained which even he did not perceive and that it had taken his little son to show it to him. Filled with great frustration, he threw down the gourd and the wisdom from it spread to all parts of the world. [1]

The moral of the story is clear: there are bits of wisdom everywhere and no one, however clever, can monopolize all knowledge, and this applies to individuals as well as to groups of individuals or human communities. Wisdom is a common heritage of humankind of which no human group is devoid, and this is regardless of their material or economic conditions, and neither does a group's technological achievement or absence of it, however that may be measured, indicate the presence or absence of wisdom in that community. An Ewe proverb aptly states that wisdom is like a baobab tree and a single man's hand cannot embrace it. [2]

This notion of wisdom in which no one person or group of persons has a monopoly, or no person or group of persons has arms long enough to embrace it, fits in well with the prevailing interest in dialogue among an increasing number of people of various faiths who are open to the enrichment of the experience and understanding of life which comes through the experience and understanding of others; and it also fits in well with our concern here at this consultation in our mutual expectation to learn from each other's perspectives, values and interpretations of experiences. An African proverb says, "It is through other people's wisdom that we learn wisdom ourselves; a single person's understanding does not amount to anything".[3] It is in a spirit of humility that this learning from the other takes place, and this further illustrates the true meaning of life as a relationship of mutually enhancing interdependence.

One may wonder how ancient wisdom, in a tradition without a written script, could be ascertained by later generations, such as those of us who are successors to the African heritage, as well as any others who may be interested in the subject. And it has not been uncommon, in the past at least, for many to conclude that in the absence of a written script there can be no authoritative or veritably reliable source of information regarding wisdom in the African tradition. But the absence of written documents is no indication or reflection of the absence of a heritage of wisdom. Every human society has a way of recording its experiences and reflections on life and passing them on down the generations, and there is an authoritative body of tradition of wisdom originating from the forebears or "glorious dead" of the society to whom the society is immeasurably indebted for its "knowledge and wisdom as well as the guarantee of authenticity to tradition".[4] This indebtedness accounts partly for the tremendous respect and veneration, oftentimes mistakenly called "ancestor worship", which the living confer on the ancestors, or as J. S. Mbiti prefers to call them, the "living-dead".[5] These "living-dead" of the society are not visions or apparitions, but are regarded as persons and are encountered as such.[6]

The recording of experiences and reflections and passing them on to succeeding generations were not only done orally (all human beings spoke before they learned to write and most of the extant cherished written traditions began as oral traditions), but also by the use of symbols and art, proverbs, folk-tales, myths, rituals, taboos, names of people, celebration of festivals and even certain social institutions. By these means, the heritage has been preserved and passed on from generation to generation. Examples of these various means of transmitting tradition will be given below, but it is sufficient at this stage to merely underscore the existence of a living tradition as a rock from which we can quarry substantial pieces of wisdom for our purpose.

Wisdom is the aggregate of all human experience and it pertains to what is true, right or lasting. Wisdom also means common sense, sagacity or good judgement as well as learning or erudition. In Akan cultural tradition, *nyansa* or wisdom is a highly prized value placed above authority, strength, size or wealth, as many folk-tales and proverbial sayings make clear. *Nyansa* is born out of the experiences in life and reflection on these experiences. *Nyansa* refers to what we have inherited from our forebears with regard to what is true, right and lasting. But it also refers to the ability to think, *dwene*, or ponder wisely about the experience of life, to find solutions to the problems of life and not merely theorize about them. *Nyansa* is practical in the sense that it is seen in what a person does and says and, the Akan have it, in the sense that wisdom is not like money to be tied up and hidden.

Nyansa normally comes with age and yet it is not necessarily restricted to the elderly. The aged have had a lot of experiences and the respect in which the old were and are still held is based on the wisdom they have acquired in life. As repositories of societal wisdom, they had the responsibility of instructing or educating the young and the right of age to instruct youth was endorsed. An Akan proverb says the words of an elder are greater than an amulet, 'opanyin ano sen suman', in other words it is better to rely on the advice of an elder (because of his or her seasoned experiences) than to place one's trust in an amulet; and furthermore, ignoring the wise counsel of an elder can lead to catastrophe.

Nyansa has a morality aspect to it, for the person who possesses wisdom knows what is right and what is wrong. In this sense, then, *nyansa* is related to character, *suban*, and the *onyansafo*, one who possesses wisdom, normally behaves in ways that enable him to live with others and to uphold the sound moral values of the society in which he or she lives. Speaking of a person with good character, the Akan could say "oye onipa", literally, "he is a real human being"; the reverse "onnye onipa", means that that person merely has put on the skin of a human being, but beneath his skin is something else.

Nyansa also means skill, learning, artfulness, knowledge, dexterity and art. The practical use or misuse of *nyansa*, in this sense, abounds in our folk-tales. Ananse, the hero in Akan folk-tales, engages in all sorts of cunning exploits aimed at obtaining his selfish ends at the expense of others, but he always comes to grief whenever he engages in these social vices. The value of such dramatization of moral conflicts is pointed out by Marcien Towa as follows:

> The very fact that a major segment of these tales dramatizes social and moral conflicts gives them a critical function within the context of traditional life; hence they become the mode of expression of an intelligence that constantly calls into question established values and institutions ... their philosophical value and status reside, therefore, in their function as a critical interrogation of the natural world and of social facts.[7]

Much of African wisdom is found in proverbs which are encapsulations of the accumulated experiences of past generations and they represent an authentic mirror of the mind of the people. They also constitute a genuine interpretation of the peoples' beliefs, principles of life and conduct.[8] Proverbs are held in high regard and according to the Zulu, "Without proverbs, the language would be but a skeleton without flesh, a body without a soul", and the Ibo say that "a child who knows how to use proverbs has justified the dowry paid on his mother's head".[9] The wise person, according to the Akan, is spoken to in proverbs, which means that he or she immediately knows and understands their meaning, whereas in the case of a fool the story is different — "when a fool is told a proverb, the meaning of it has to be explained to him".

I set out a few proverbs about wisdom:

The wise person who does not learn ceases to be wise.

If you say you know everything, you will sleep in a fool's hallway.

A fool's walking stick helps the wise person to stand. Where you cheat a fool, a wise man sits and watches. [10]

The main thrust of this paper is the African perception of wisdom relating to what is true, right and lasting but does not attempt to embrace the baobab tree of wisdom in its totality in the African heritage. In referring to the wisdom heritage in Africa, it is not necessarily being implied that a certain minimal complex of significant elements which are common to African cultures are such that they have never been seen elsewhere before in the history of mankind. Only a few alternatives face mankind at the level of fundamentals and it should come as no surprise to us that at some time, somewhere outside the African environment, a people have explained or understood things in ways fundamentally identical to those in Africa. [11]

But there is an essentially African approach or understanding of some fundamental questions and truths which grow out of our own environment here on this continent. Busia wrote:

Every culture represents unique answers by a people to certain universal questions in the context of a particular historical situation, particular resources, skills, and knowledge. Every group finds itself in a natural environment that offers possibilities for, as well as sets limits on, the provision of food, shelter, clothing, and the fulfilment of other human wants. According to the available knowledge, the group finds its own solutions to the universal problems posed by its basic material needs. These solutions, the answers it adopts, are aspects of its culture — as are the group's solutions to the problems of law and the ordering of human relations in social organisations and political systems, to the problems of human intercourse in language and art, song and dance, and to the problems that grow from man's deeper cravings, his need for mental and spiritual expression in ethics, philosophy, and religion, according to the group's concepts of the universe and men's place and purpose in it. [12]

The world view

African views of the universe [13] or all existing things, are born out of centuries of experience and mature reflection on those experiences. The universe did not come into existence of its own volition but was brought into being or created by the Creator. Many names for God in African languages mean Creator, e.g. Akan: Oboadee — Creator; Bini: Osanobua — Creator of the world, sky and earth; Ibo: Chineke — Creator; Ijaw: Ayiba — Maker of souls; Yoruba: Eleda — the Creator, the Maker. Other names refer to the Creator as Moulder, Hewer, Excavator, Originator, Carver and Artist-in-Chief. [14] That everything that is was created by the

Creator or God, however he is envisaged, is the most fundamental assumption in African cosmology, and it is a statement accepted or supposed to be true and which requires neither proof nor demonstration.

Through the use of myths, the truth about the nature and origin of the universe has passed down through the ages from generation to generation and these myths are no longer regarded by serious-minded scholars as outworn or risible products of primitive imagination which held sway in the absence of scientific truth. On the contrary, as a scholar of the study of religion recently put it:

> … myth expresses profound and multidimensional truth. Far from being those outworn stories that are inherently false, myths are, to me, those timeless stories that are inherently true. They are true not because they "happened" once, but because they go on happening every day. They shape the ways in which we think about our place in the cosmos and our relation to the Divine. To come to know a people — and that includes ourselves as well — is to know their stories, especially their "true stories" or myths. [15]

In the African creation myths, it is obvious that the universe had a clear beginning but there is no indication of an end to it in African cosmological thought. This is due to the postulate of God as a supreme deity who created and sustains all things. An Akan maxim which is hallowed by the wisdom and the tradition of the elders is, "obi nkyere abofra Nyame" — "no one points out God to a child". By this, the Akan meant that the existence of God is immediate and self-evident and one does not even need to point it out to a child. This postulate is continent-wide and is part of the tradition which is handed down.

This Supreme Deity, who goes by many names, [16] is eternal and the act of upholding the universe is an unending, eternal, activity of the Creator. Since the Creator sustains the universe, there is no thought that it will come to an end. To show him as sustainer or protector of the universe, a few West African names may be cited: Mebee (Bulu, Cameroon) — the one who bears the world; Osebuluwa (Ibo, Nigeria) — the Lord who upholds the world; Egbesu (Ijaw, Nigeria) — Supreme Protector. Some proverbial sayings also confirm the sustaining activity of the Creator in relation to the universe. The Ibo say, "If God removes his hand the world will end" [17] and the Bam-buti of the Congo affirm that "If God should die, the world would also collapse". [18]

That the idea that the universe is unending is not a mere theoretical assertion in the African cultural tradition was expressed by Mbiti in the following words:

> The idea that the universe has no ending is also depicted in rituals and art forms by African peoples. For example, the drawing of snakes with their tails in their mouths symbolize the unending universe. There are many rituals all over Africa that celebrate and re-enact the rhythm of birth — death — and rebirth. Thus, in African views, the universe is permanent, unending, and eternal. God sustains it. There is no reason to imagine that it will ever end, let alone how that such an ending would come about as the universe is sustained by God who Himself is everlasting. [19]

Furthermore, there is in the beliefs in an unending universe the reflection of a deep faith in God that he will not destroy what he has created and that he continues to sustain, uphold and bear his creation. This faith partly accounts for some attitudes towards nature which border on reverence found in African communities.

But God appears to be far removed from his creation, and much of the early writing on Africa gave the interminable impression that the Creator in Africa retired into the heavens or wherever he is imagined to be living, since he was unwilling to be bothered by the troubles of mankind. Moreover, many African myths which tell of separation between the heaven and the earth, or the 'withdrawal' of God from human society, seem to lend further credence to this impression. Abraham recounts an Akan myth thus:

> ... once upon a time, when our ancestors were young, God lived very close to us. One day, however, a certain old woman, who was pounding *her fufu* [a plantain meal] with pestle and mortar, struck heaven with her pestle. Whereupon God said to her: "Why do you do this to me? Because of what you have done, I am taking myself far up". And, true to his word, as was to be expected, God betook himself far up ... The old woman, regretting that God was no longer near to man, asked all her children to gather together all the mortars they could find and, by building them one upon another, reach up to God on high. The children were dutiful enough, but found that they were one mortar short. The old woman ... having taken thought, spoke again thus: "Children, remove the bottom-most mortar, and by placing it on the top one so reach God at last." Once more the dutiful children did as they were bidden. But now all the mortars collapsed, rolled to the ground, and all the children perished. [20]

Myths from other parts of Africa speak of a hyena biting the rope that linked the heavens with the earth, thus bringing about a separation, or a woman with dirty fingers touching the sky which was so close to the earth that human beings could stretch their hands and pluck bits of it for food. The contact with the dirty fingers caused the heavens to remove themselves away from men.

These myths tell a universal truth about man; briefly put, man is not self-sufficient and needs God for fulfilment. If man were self-sufficient, he would have no need for religion. Even though the myths give the impression of a time of completeness, self-sufficiency or primordial bliss, their intention is not to bemoan the loss of this age of innocence. Quite the contrary, the separation or withdrawal signifies the beginning of religion, for God or the heavens have to be at a distance, from the earth or man, before communication can be possible. As Zahan elucidates it:

> All African ritual practices concerning rainbow, clouds, and rain are based on the "distance" which separates the sky and the earth. Similarly, all relations between the Creator and created is acknowledged. Thus, far from representing an action which unfolds two eras, paradisiac life and fall, these themes contain the element which establishes the possibility of religion as communication: distance. In other words, in order to understand the significance of these mythical accounts it is necessary to reverse what they seem to

suggest at first glance. The period of man's "religiousness" is not at all the "paradisiac" era when God lived in the "village" of men, but the period following, when God had lost his earthly and human qualities in order to live separately from mankind.[21]

But where the idea of separation is implied, it is the otherness of God that is being alluded to and not God's physical separation. God is above his creation and is at the same time involved in his creation by upholding the universe, creating the children that are born to people, and is involved in the daily lives of men. Two Ibo proverbs say "*God* owns a person lost in the woods", i.e. God takes care of the person lost in the woods; and "Whoever wants to do evil to another, does not remember God",[22] meaning God constantly watches over men and takes account of whatever people do. Many personal names which incorporate the name of God in the local languages also reinforce the involvement of God in the lives of people. Olufemi (Yoruba) — God loves me; Chukuemeka (Ibo) — God has done much; Seloame (Ewe) — the Creator loves mankind, or God is kind to people.

Origin of man and the human community

Man is understood to be a created being and there are mythological accounts of his origin which make him come out of a hole in the ground or out of a bed of reeds,[23] from the sky, from clay which the Creator kneaded or, as the Fulani myth tells it, out of stone, iron, fire, water and air.[24] Human beings were usually created in couples at the same time (as in the Dogon myth where the Creator kneaded two balls of clay and out of the balls emerged male and female), not female after male, which has enormous possibilities for teaching equality of the sexes in the sense that the female was not created as an afterthought and that the complementary roles of male and female are grounded in the self-understanding of man. Human beings also appear in groups in other myths, an idea which undergirds the notion of community so prevalent in Africa.

Every human being, according to the Akan of Ghana, possesses an *okra*, the aspect of Onyame, God, in every person, which is the essential part of being human. Animals do not possess *okra*. The *okra* is divine in origin and has an ante-mundane existence as well as post-mundane existence. There is therefore a direct relationship between God and man, and death is signified by the return of the *okra* to its source, hence the Akan saying, "Onyame bewu na mawu", literally, "could God die, I will die" or, "I shall only die if God dies", which is a reference to the *okra*, the undying part of the human person. It is inconceivable to the Akan to imagine that the Creator could die and therefore the *okra* does not die when one dies physically. An Akan maxim also epigramatically expresses the idea that when a person dies he is not (really) dead — "onipa wu a na onwui". In other words, there is something which is eternal and indestructible in man which continues to live in the land of the spirits. Furthermore, everyone is unique and has worth deriving from the Creator.

Myths about death have a level of profundity at which they clearly inform us about the conception of the human condition held by the narrators of the myths. In some of the myths human beings did not have a choice, but in others, however, they had a choice between immortality and mortality, and they chose the latter. A Nupe (Nigeria) myth recounts:

> In the beginning God created tortoises, men and stones and, with the exception of the stones, he made them male and female and provided them with life. However, none of the species reproduced. One day the tortoise wanted to have descendants and asked this of God, whose response was that he had granted life to the tortoise and to men but had not given them permission to have children. At this time the story adds, men did not die; when they became old they were automatically rejuvenated. The tortoise renewed his appeal and God warned against the danger of death which would result from a positive response on his part. But the tortoise took no notice and pressed his request. He was joined by men, who had decided to have children even at the risk of death, while the stones refused to join in with them. Thus God granted tortoises and men the ability to have posterity, and death entered the world, but the stones remained unaffected. [25]

The choice of mortality clearly affirms our nature as human beings and the contrary would have led to a rejection of the human condition. It needs to be noted here that death did not come as a consequence of human sin and that, in African views, death does not terminate life since man has a spark or portion of the divine in him which is not subject to the destructive forces of death. Death is not the opposite of life, in reality the opposite of death is birth; as death takes away members from the community, birth makes up for the losses inflicted on the community. Such ideas are not intended to encourage the illusion of escaping the reality of death:

> … on the contrary, while living in full awareness of our mortality, we are provided with its real meaning and significance within the context of the totality of human life, as well as with the tools to overcome our mortality. The genius of the African humanity reveals itself in the ideas about death and immortality even when we live in full cognizance of the transcience of bodily existence. Life is not restricted to bodily existence, for the soul which is distinct from the body and which is identified with the conscious self continues to live after the death and disintegration of the physical body. [26]

Communalism and community

One of the most vital features of the African heritage is the sense of community. The community has a religious foundation and goes beyond the limits of its visible members to include God, regarded by the Akan as the First Grand Ancestor of the community, [27] or the Overlord of the community, the ancestors who are the forebears of the community and who uphold communal unity and co-operation, as well as those yet to be born.

Traditional education gives primary place to personal relations and to be human is to be in relation not only with members of one's family, clan or community, but also with the spiritual beings as well as with nature. The importance of relationships lies in the fact that each person shares in common familyhood with all others — those who are dead, those who are alive and those who are to be born. The community is therefore an integrated entity which is undergirded and kept alive by extended relationships, the purpose of which is to enhance unity and promote greater and friendly co-operation.

The emphasis on co-operation, mutual helpfulness, concern for group welfare as virtues which are fundamental to the community ideal and are worthy of pursuit is based on the assumption that life's meaning is realized when an individual is a member of a group or community.

It would appear that such emphasis on group life threatens the idea of individualism and that the individual is sacrificed to group interest. But in the African view of things, the needs and interest of all the members of the community can best be taken care of by a system of communalism, which is geared towards the promotion of the general welfare and interest of all the individual members who belong to the community. Promoting group interest does not necessarily lead to the denial or abrogation of the individual's interest, for it is argued that the well-being of the group cannot be considered in isolation from that of the individual. For man by nature cannot live outside society. An Akan maxim states, "onipa fi soro besi a, obesi nnipa kurom" — "when a man descends from heaven, he descends into a human society". This maxim merely underscores the belief that man is social by nature and that it is therefore not possible for him to live in isolation because he is not born to live a life of solitariness, and society is the context or condition for human existence. Besides, man as an individual is not self-sufficient to the extent that all his basic needs could be met by him alone, the assistance of others, in order to satisfy one's basic needs, is required and the lack of self-sufficiency in man is given expression by the maxim which contrasts the self-sufficiency of the palm kernel, which is covered by a hard shell, with the human person who is not — "onipa nnye abe, na ne ho ahyia ne ho" — "man is not a palm kernel that he should be self-sufficient". Furthermore, one needs to be in relation with others in order to realize one's full personality

The recognition or awareness that man is not self-sufficient is not a denial of human possibilities; on the contrary, human possibilities are enhanced when they are linked with those of others in community. Co-operation, mutual help and collective action are the *sine qua non* of individual welfare and, moreover, they make possible the achievement of undertakings which might appear to be difficult. An Ibo proverb puts the matter this way: "If anyone thinks that to go in pairs [co-operate with each other] is not useful, let him hold his upper lip and see whether the lower one can speak alone".

The individual and his relationship to society is symbolized in Akan art by a Siamese crocodile,[28] with two heads, two tails and a common stomach, and the saying that goes with it is that although they have a common stomach they struggle over food (as if the food were going into different or separate stomachs). The two crocodiles have separate heads, and each member of society has a uniqueness of his own, which is given expression in individual tastes, wishes, passions and desires. These differ from person to person and constitute individual self-expression, and it is because the crocodiles have separate heads that conflicts over food arise. In the same way, conflicts in human society arise because of the individuality of its members. The symbol gives recognition to human individuality but goes on to suggest the background against which conflicts which arise out of personal individuality may be viewed.

The crocodiles have a common stomach and this indicates that members of the community share an identity of interests and this common interest is the result of the co-operation of all. The contribution of each leads to the good of all and the symbol depicts the futility of social conflicts. The co-operation of all the members ensures the prosperity of all.

Community with nature

Ideas about community are not restricted to the community of human beings. In a much larger sense, man's life is intimately bound up with nature, which is the irreplaceable basis of life. Man is part of nature and is expected to co-operate with it. Nature is not regarded as "other" but as an integral part of man's world order.[29] Quite apart from providing sustenance for man, nature provides a model, a source of wisdom for the resolution of conflicts in human society as well as a basis for man's self-understanding. The relationship with nature is often expressed in terms of identity and kinship, friendliness and respect, and this attitude is based on faith in the goodness of the goal of nature. But man makes use of nature even though nature is also revered.

Features of the environment are often personified in the African tradition and this is a way of keeping a harmonious relationship between man and his environment, as well as a way of preserving nature. Many taboos regarding man's relations with nature are an attempt to preserve nature. An African consultation report stated, among other things:

> ... our concept of taboo as a ritual prohibition is designed to protect nature; its violation calls for restitution to be made to nature. Humanity is at the centre of the cosmos, not in a self-appointed or self-assertive role, but in a dependent, caretaker role, for its life depends on cosmic harmony being maintained. Nature is therefore not just an object but a tangible reality from which humanity derives its sense of wholeness and well-being.[30]

A ritual observance by fishermen in Ghana may be noted. It is demanded by tradition that fishermen must "sacrifice" some of their catch to Bosompo, the god of the sea, after each fishing expedition before returning home. The fish that are sacrificed must be live fish, not dead ones, and an Akan maxim which supports this ritual says: "Bosompo ankame wo nam a, nso wonkame no abia" — "if the god of the sea does not begrudge you of his fish, you do not begrudge him of your catch". The fish which fishermen "sacrifice" to Bosompo will continue to breed and there will continue to be fish in the ocean, if this ritual is observed. It is therefore taboo for a fisherman not to make a "sacrifice" and the concern for the environment expressed in the ritual sacrifice is quite evident.

In the farming areas, too, it is taboo for anyone to bring back home a whole bunch of palm fruits from the farm. One is expected by custom to cut a bit of the palm fruits and leave the nuts in the forest before returning home. The idea behind this is that every palm fruit which is brought home is going to be boiled or cooked and the kernels will not germinate. But the palm fruits left in the farm or forest will germinate and grow into palm trees and provide food not only for the present generation but also for future generations. Those who did not observe this taboo were regarded as a threat to human society and were dealt with accordingly in the past.

The importance of the taboo is not diminished by the argument that squirrels and crows which feed on ripe palm fruits do propagate the seeds and therefore render the taboo of no consequence in 'modern' times. But this argument ignores the fact of human responsibility towards the environment which is inherent in the taboo. It is not the responsibility of squirrels and crows, or for that matter, any other animals, to ensure human survival and ecological balance. It is man's responsibility and that is why infringement of the taboo is taken seriously. And it is clear that the observance of this taboo is an expression of concern for the environment and its preservation.

Expression of values

Mention has already been made of the means employed by Africans to transmit wisdom and values down the ages and a few examples will now be given.

Proverbs are a vehicle for the expression of values, as we have pointed out and a few of these relating to other cherished values may be given.

If God gives you a goblet of wine, and a living man kicks it down, *God* makes it up to the brim for you.

If the plucky sparrow got nothing else from God, it got dash (i.e. there is no creature without a particular gift from God).

Says the hawk: "All God created is good".

Whereas a liar takes a thousand years to go on a journey, the one who speaks the truth follows and overtakes the liar in a day.

If you travel with fraud, you may reach your destination but will be unable to return.

Those who are the cause of their own troubles never come to the end of them; but those who are troubled by other people do.

It is one's deeds that are counted, not one's years.

If your parents take care of you until you finish teething, you take care of them when they lose theirs.

If a quantity of water does not suffice for a bath, it will at least be sufficient for drinking.

When the state begins to collapse, the cause can be found in the home. The warrior fights with courage, not with excessive anger.

When deeds speak, words are nothing.

Life is riches.

Art is used to express social values and philosophico-religious ideas. Among the regalia used by Akan chiefs in Ghana are linguist staffs with carved emblems on top of them. Among these may be found a human hand holding an egg.[31] This expresses the idea that power must be handled in the manner of holding an egg in the hand: if you hold it too firmly it breaks, if you hold it too loosely it drops. And to underscore the value of gratitude and warn against ingratitude, there is the carving of a cock or hen standing by its water basin, looking into the sky and this says that the cock in drinking water raises its head to God in thankfulness.

Even textile designs convey essential or important values. The indestructibility of the human soul is depicted in the *adinkra* cloth in Ghana by a symbol stamped on the cloth[32] which says "I shall only die if God dies", and another symbol, Gye Nyame,[33] expresses the omnipotence of God.

Designs woven into the *kente* cloth also express cherished values. It may be mentioned in this connection that the kente cloth presented by Ghana on the occasion of its admission into the membership of the United Nations in 1957 is called "Ti koro nko agyina" — "one head does riot go into council", in other words, it takes more than one head to arrive at a sound decision. Another way of putting it is, wisdom does not reside in one person's head.

Conclusion

The foregoing gives us a glimpse into some aspects of the heritage of wisdom in Africa and the many ways in which it has been preserved and handed down from generation to generation. It offers alternative approaches to human experience but in quite a number of instances there are convergences with insights and experiences found elsewhere. In a world whose moral and intellectual inadequacies are more than self-evident and in which we see an increasing secularization of society at the expense of the metaphysical dimension of society, Busia's reflections on the sense of dependence on the spiritual powers in all religious observances in Africa vis-a-vis the technological competence of modern man are worth considering. He wrote:

A consciousness of the inadequacy and incompleteness of man and of his inability to cope successfuly with life without supernatural aid stands out prominently in prayer and ritual. This may be seized upon as proof of the primitiveness of the African, since there are those who contend that the difference between primitive man and civilized man is that the latter, through the competence which his technology gives him, is able to exercise control over his natural environment, and is therefore much more independent. It is true that technology increases man's control over nature, and gives him greater independence.

But there is much more to the consciousness of inadequacy and dependence manifest in African religious rites; it implies a philosophy of man which sees him as a created being dependent on his Creator. This recognition is essential to the religious life and is not altered by man's increasing technological competence. [34]

It may be worth our while to remember the symbolism of the giant baobab tree whose trunk no man's arms can completely embrace and discover our need for each other and our mutual interdependence.

As we engage in dialogue, we participate in the worthwhile and urgent endeavour to create a new world of harmony and equilibrium where each contributes his irreplaceable values for the benefit of all. In the end, we need to realize that we form one human community on the face of the earth and that we need each other's insights in order to be able to live in community. This realization will lead to the humility which will regard truth not as a possession already in our hands but rather as a horizon towards which we are moving. [35]

Kofi Asare Opoku

NOTES

[1] R. S. Rattray, *Akan-Ashanti Folk-Tales* (Oxford 1969), 5-7; also Kofi Asare Opoku, *Speak to the Winds: Proverbs from Africa* (New York 1975), 8-10.

[2] See N. K Dzobo, *African Proverbs: Guide to Conduct* (Accra 1975).

[3] Opoku, 19.

[4] Dominique Zahan, *The Religion, Spirituality and Thought of Traditional Africa* (Chicago 1970), 51 (originally published as *Religion, spiritualité et pensées africaines* (Paris 1970)).

[5] See his *African Religions and Philosophy* (London 1969), 25ff.

[6] See Gabriel Setiloane, *African Theology: An Introduction* (Johannesburg 1986), 18.

[7] In *L'idée d'une philosophie africaine* (Yaoundé 1979), as quoted by Abiola Irele in "Contemporary thought in French-speaking Africa" in I. J. Mowoe and R. Bjornsen (eds.), *Africa and the West: The Legacies of Empire* (New York 1986), 145.

[8] Emefie Ikenga Metuh, *African Religions in Western Conceptual Schemes — The Problem of Interpretation* (Bodija 1985), 23.

[9] *Ibid.*

[10] For more African proverbs, see R. S. Rattray, *Ashanti Proverbs* (Oxford 1916); G. Barra, *One Thousand Kikuyu Proverbs* (London 1960); Isaac O. Delano, *Owe L'Esen Oro* (London 1966).

[11] W. E. Abraham, *The Mind of Africa* (London 1962), 115.

[12] K. A. Busia, *The Challenge of Africa* (New York 1962), 40.

[13] For a specific treatment of an African worldview, see Kofi Asare Opuku, "The world-view of the Akan" in *Tarikh* 26, vol. 7, no. 2 (published for the Historical Society of Nigeria by Longman, 1982), 61-73.

[14] See Mbiti, esp. chapter 5.

[15] Diana Eck, 'The perspective of pluralism in theological education' in Sam Amirtham and S. Wesley Ariarajah (eds), *Ministerial Formation in a Multi-Faith Milieu* (Geneva 1986), 60.

[16] See J. S. Mibiti, *Concepts of God in Africa* (London 1970).

[17] Metuh, 25.

[18] Mbiti, *African Religions*, 42.

[19] "African cosmology" in *Festac 77* (Lagos African Journal Limited, London and International Festival Committee), 44.

[20] *Ibid.*, 54.

[21] *Ibid.*, 16.

[22] Metuh, 25.

[23] Setiloane, 3-5; see also Mbiti, *African Religions*, 92-9.

[24] As quoted by J. S. Mbiti in Mowoe and Bjornsen, 57.

[25] Leo Frobenius, *Atlantis* (Jena), vol. 12, 1928, 140 as quoted by Zahan, 41.

[26] Kofi Asare Opoku, "Death and immortality in the African religious heritage" (Calabar 1984). For a discussion of contemporary ideas on death and survival, see David Lorimer, *Survival? Body, Mind and Death in the Light of Psychic Experience* (London 1984), esp. 9-28.

[27] J. B. Danquah, *Akan Doctrine of God* (second ed.) (London 1968).

[28] See illustration on page 57.

[29] E. Obiechina, *Culture, Tradition and Society in the West African Novel* (Cambridge 1975), 42.

[30] *Religious Experience in Humanity's Relation with Nature: A Consultation* (Yaounde, Cameroon/Geneva 1978), 14.

[31] See illustration on page 57.

[32] See illustration on page 57.

[33] See illustration on page 57.

[34] K. A. Busia, "The religious heritage" in *The African Consciousness: Continuity and Change in Africa* (New York: American African Affairs Association, 1968), 7.

[35] Kofi Asare Opoku, "Communalism and community in Africa" in C. D. Jathanna (ed.), *Dialogue in Community* (essay in honour of S. J. Samartha) (Balmatta, Mangalore: Karnataka Theological Research Institute, 1982), 160.

The Biblical understanding of creation and the human commitment

Introduction

Two weeks ago, Jews all over the world observed Rosh Hashanah, the festival which marks the beginning of the new year. A Jewish tradition ascribed to Rabbi Eliezer ben Hyrcanus (second century CE) has it that this season coincides with the time of the year in which creation occurred.[1] This synchronization highlights the idea that creation merges at some juncture with history, actually leading into metahistory, and thus can still be observed in human experience. This linking of history with creation reflects the concept of a *creatio continua*, which is debated by Jewish thinkers, and not by them alone.

I see in this understanding of creation flowing into history an expression of the meaning which can be attached to creation as a guideline for human commitment to principles of individual and societal behaviour, such as can be extrapolated from the biblical traditions concerning the beginning of the world.

The linkage of creation with history by having the beginning of the world coincide with the beginning of the calendar year was accentuated in a dissident Jewish tradition, which came to our knowledge barely forty years ago. I refer to the discovery in the Judaean Desert of ancient manuscripts constituting the "Library of the Covenanters of Qumran".[2] An investigation of the ingenious solar-lunar calendar of 364 days to which the Covenanters adhered shows that the first day of their year always fell on the day on which God is said to have created the great luminaries (Genesis 1:16).[3] There can be little doubt that in this instance the synchronization of the flow of time in the actual life of the individual and of society is highlighted by harnessing the calendar to the timetable of the biblical creation story. Thus history is riveted to a time-pattern which was divinely established for eternity from the very beginning of the world.

A dual approach

The first part of my presentation is determined by the exegetical methods developed and perfected in contemporary biblical scholarship. Here we bring under scrutiny a variety of creation traditions present in Hebrew scriptures, albeit only in bits and pieces. On that level of analysis, one may expect a high degree of similarity both in techniques and in results at which scholars arrive, irrespective of their creed or confession:

objectivity, determined by scientific reasoning, outweighs or should out-
weigh subjectivity.

The restrictions imposed upon the scholar by the demand for objectivity become less stringent when he or she approaches the problem of
creation as an interpreter, who aims to extrapolate from the biblical tradition guidelines for human behaviour in the present time. At this stage
of the investigation, he or she necessarily speaks 'from within the credal
fold' of his or her persuasion and is actually called upon to bring into
play his or her religious beliefs. In doing so, he or she will be integrated
into the ongoing process of interpretation of the basic biblical texts as it
has developed over the ages in that particular tradition. Therefore, in the
second part of my deliberations, speaking as a *Jewish* Bible scholar,
I shall direct my remarks exclusively to the creation story in the book of
Genesis which became normative in Jewish tradition. Only in passing
shall I mention residues of and allusions to other biblical depictions of
creation, which reflect ancient Near Eastern myths which were still current among the Hebrews and which had trickled into their cultural heritage and sacred writings.

While it is desirable to separate the *objective* approach from the *subjective*, it would be preposterous to maintain that this separation can
always be neatly achieved. At times, the realm of scholarly objectivity
may be invaded by subjective ideological or religious considerations
which arise from the *condition humaine*. This seems to be acceptable as
long as the merging occurs under control, that is to say, as long as subjective interpretation is not given full dominance over scholarly objectivity, thus turning the exegesis of biblical texts into eisegesis.

The duality of approaches outlined above is linked with two further
phenomena which must be taken into account. One pertains to the
matter under investigation, the other to the investigator.

Fragmentary information

We should first highlight a difficulty which confronts the student of
the Hebrew scriptures, irrespective of his credal affiliation: the principles and concepts which supposedly inspired the factual events which
predominate in biblical literature are never fully explicated. Rarely, if
ever, does a biblical author present his reflections on such matters in a
systematic fashion and in abstract conceptual terms. Scholars have
called attention to the narrative-dramatic tenor of the biblical Creation
account and the concomitant paucity of abstract vocables in the biblical
as well as in the post-biblical Hebrew vocabulary pertaining to Creation.[4]

From this results a dilemma, common to the experience of all students
of the Hebrew Bible: the scholar who sets out to present an integrated
picture of any aspect in the biblical world of ideas must resort to con-
joining fragmentary bits of mostly factual information, extracted from a
diversity of texts. Conceptualization does not surface in the texts themselves, but rather can be achieved, to a restricted degree, by the scholar's

endeavour to distil from the reported 'facts' elements which will assist him or her in revealing the presumed cogitation and conceptualization of the ancient writers. But the result of this labour will always be a mosaic in which many pieces are missing. [5]

The problem of relating ideas to actualities

The Jewish scholar faces an additional limitation which impedes any attempt to delineate the specifically Jewish appreciation of conceptual matters pertaining to the Bible, such as the understanding of Creation and the imperatives of human commitment which can be elicited from it. Judaism is not monolithic in the interpretation of its heritage. The varying interpretations of Creation to a large degree depend directly on the specific historical situation in which an interpretation is offered. The application of biblical ideas to the changing realities of successive generations of Jewish thinkers bears the imprint of contemporary political-religious conditions. It follows that, in an attempt to define the essence of Jewish understanding of Creation, selection is imperative. Even then, what will emerge is the view of a Jew and not of Jewish tradition in its comprehensiveness. Therefore, one can only hope to recapture some pivotal aspects which guide, or should guide, Jewish thinking on Creation and on its demands on human commitment in the present age.

Judaism, or Jews, diverged and still diverges from — and sometimes flagrantly flouts — the principles which can seemingly be distilled from the basic normative sources of the Hebrew Bible. Reality seldom dovetails with ideal concepts which bear upon them the stamp of Utopia.

The biblical rejection of pagan mythology

The biblical Creation tradition, not unlike cosmogonies which were transmitted by diverse people in many cultures all over the world, gives expression to a pre- or proto-scientific endeavour on the part of men of faith to fathom the quintessence of the universe, chart the place of man in it and define the tasks and functions allotted to him. By the nature of things, this tradition necessarily has a retrospective thrust. It may enlighten us on the understanding and the intellectual stance of the biblical author or authors, rather than reveal the factualities of Creation which remained hidden to the ancients, not less and possibly even more than to modern man.

It is from here that any attempt to define a human commitment to Creation in the framework of the Jewish, and similarly in the Christian, world of ideas must take its departure. It should be stressed that, like its ensuing interpretation in post-biblical Judaism, as has been widely illustrated elsewhere, scriptural tradition concerning Creation is not monolithic. The major tradition is embedded in the first part of the book of Genesis, which, as will be seen below, is itself considered to be composite. But there are also echoes of ancient Near Eastern tales of creation, residues of ancient cosmogonies which had been current in

Mesopotamia and the Canaanite expanse on the coast of the Mediterranean. Of special importance in this respect are echoes of epic texts found fifty years ago at Minet-el-Baida, a small seaside town on the Phoenician coast. Until the thirteenth century BCE, the kingdom of Ugarit occupied this territory. The geographical proximity of the site, and the linguistic similarity of the Ugaritic (West Semitic) language and biblical Hebrew facilitated the absorption of Ugaritic phraseology and imagery into ancient Israelite literature. The pagan substance of the epic works was rejected by the biblical authors, in whose writings they play only a minor role and require only cursory attention; the mythological residues pertain predominantly to two features of ancient cosmogony.

There are recurring references in diverse biblical books and literary genres to a creator deity who battles against forces that oppose him in the act of creation, represented by primordial monsters: Mot, lord of the netherworld, and his allies — Yam, Tiamat-Sheol, Leviathan, Rahab, the Rigid (or Fleeing) Serpent and others. These residues, in fact, highlight the impotence of the fiends when their futile opposition is viewed in the framework of the monotheistic biblical tradition of the acts of the sole and sovereign Creator God. In Job 7:8, we read "He [who] alone stretched out the skies, trampled upon Yam's carcass"; or, again, in Job 26:12-14, "With his might he subdued Yam, with his wisdom he crushed Rahab, with his will he fashioned heavens, his hand transfixed the rigid [fleeing] serpent"; and, in Psalm 74:13-14, "By your power you split Yam, you smashed the heads of the Taninim upon the waters, you crushed Leviathan's heads".

Similar terminology is used in passages in which the writer entreats God to re-enact his victory over inimical powers in future battles against them. For example, in Isaiah 27:1, "That day, YHWH, with his hard sword, massive and strong, will bring punishment upon Leviathan, the rigid [fleeing] serpent, and upon Leviathan the bent [twisting] serpent, he will kill the Tanin of Yam [the sea]."

It can confidently be surmised that all these references had already lost their original pagan content and that the biblical writers employed mythological terminology as a figure of speech, drawing from a storehouse of well-known Canaanite or, rather, ancient Semitic mythopoeic phraseology. This is borne out by the fact that the same terminology is also employed on a quite different plane by biblical writers who implore God to vanquish in history his enemies, who are the enemies of Israel, as we see in Isaiah 51:9, "Arise, arise! Clothe yourself in strength, arm of YHWH, arise as in the past, in times long ago, when you transfixed Rahab, pierced Tanin, dried up the Sea [Yam], the water of the great abyss [Tehom — Tiamat]".

It is of interest to observe that such borrowed mythopoeic imagery is found mainly in prophetic and wisdom literature and in Psalms, in which poetic licence facilitates its use. It is practically absent from biblical historiography and also from the Pentateuch, in which historical narratives and legal materials preponderate. The one mention of Taninim in the normative Creation tradition in the book of Genesis actually substantiates the claim that this mythopoeic terminology had lost it cosmogonic connotations for the Hebrews. The primordial monsters who, in mythology, could oppose the creator-deity, in the biblical tradition are denigrated to the status of creatures which, like all creatures, were sovereignly fashioned by the one and only God: in Genesis 1:21, "He created the great Taninim and every kind of living creature with which the waters teem."

Mark the insistence on referring to these presumed primordial deities in the plural, thus denying to them their original "divine" singularity. Their reduction to mere creatures is further developed in God's famous answer to Job, who rebelled against the injustice that he had suffered: no human has a right to question the mystery of the acts of God, who alone created the world. In this context, the ancient myth of a primordial monster opposing the creator-deity is given a most interesting twist: the "mighty Leviathan" is turned into a pet that can be paraded in public.

> Can you catch Leviathan with a fish hook or put a line through his tongue? Can you put a ring through his nose, or pierce his jaw with a hook? Will he plead and plead with you, will he coax you with smooth words? Will he make an agreement with you to become your eternal slave? Will you play with him like [with a] pet bird, tie him on a leash for [the amusement] of your maids [Job 40:25-9]?[6]

It is also probable that the portrayal of the snake in the garden of Eden, which cunningly persuades man to violate the Creator's commandments and in punishment is reduced to "eating dust" (Genesis 3:1-15), is meant to ridicule the primordial serpent which dared to oppose the mythological divine creator.

The biblical garden of Eden story may actually be another adjusted ancient Near Eastern mythological tale. What looks like an early pagan version of the Genesis account is still preserved in an oracle against the King of Tyre in the book of Ezekiel (28:11-19). The king is depicted strutting proudly among sundry precious stones which abound in God's "garden of Eden", located on God's "holy mountain" (Ezekiel 28:13, 14). This conception was corrected in the Genesis version of the Eden story, in which the garden is established from the outset to house man, whom God puts there to "cultivate and take care of it" (Genesis 2:15). Here, normal vegetation replaces the almost mythical abundance of precious stones in the version which is given in Ezekiel (this motif can be seen in Genesis 2:12): the human king of Tyre, swollen with pride, aspires to become godlike, saying, "I am sitting on the throne of God" (Ezekiel 28:2). He considers himself "an exemplar of perfection, full of wisdom, perfect in beauty" and actually wishes to play the role of the "guardian cherub" in charge of the mythical garden (compare Ezekiel 28:12-14 with Genesis 3:24 and 2:15). How different the depiction of Adam and Eve, man and wife, in the Hebrew version: man and wife whom God had placed in the garden of Eden for their own enjoyment (Genesis 3:1-20). Both Adam and the King of Tyre are punished for their transgressions: one, for disobeying a divine command; the other, for his overbearing hubris, his aspiring to divinity. The first is condemned to live in the realism of human life, toiling with sweat on his brow to win sustenance from the soil to which he will return after death (Genesis 3:17-19); the other is consumed by a fire bursting forth from his own body (Ezekiel 28:18). The message seems to be obvious: myth is rejected by means of completely revamping its essential content and by substituting human-existential reality for mythic imagery.

As a result of this "watering down", such literary residues which give evidence to the currency of pagan mythology in ancient Israel in some instances could be combined with references to the normative Hebrew tradition of Creation. For example, God's above-mentioned reply to Job's complaints brims with mythological imagery (Job 40, 41), but preceding this, we find God rejecting Job's rebellious outcries by referring to Creation in terms which clearly echo the Creation pericope in Genesis 1 (Job 38, 39; compare also Job 38:5 with Isaiah 41:12, 22).

The biblical account of Creation

We can now turn our attention to an analysis and evaluation of the normative Hebrew Creation tradition in Genesis 1-2. In modern biblical research it is commonly agreed that the pericope is composite. Even though traditional scholars, both Christians and Jews, insist that this pericope is a unit, differences in language and content leave little doubt that indeed the passage is made up of originally independent Creation accounts.

There have been various ways of identifying its major components but the overwhelming majority of scholars would ascribe one account to the priestly source (P) and the other to the yahwistic source (J). However, for our present considerations, the division is of little consequence. We have to relate to the text as it is, taking a holistic approach, somewhat along the lines set by the emerging new school of "canonical criticism".

The question that confronts us is this: what is the message which the final arranger of the pericope wished to convey to his audience? The answer is obvious. The biblical account of Creation, in all its presumed subdivisions, propounds one pivotal idea: the universe was established by a sole and sovereign Creator, who went about his task unaided by any helpers and unimpeded by any opposing forces. The biblical text, though, does not offer any help for solving a problem which has exercised the minds of later theologians and philosophers: is the formation of the universe viewed as c*reatio ex nihilo* or does the account rather conceive of the creator as giving form to pre-existing matter? The Hebrew Bible simply relates facts, and not all facts, and does not interpret them. To a degree this method of a factual presentation of "events" is followed by most later Jewish commentators, theologians and philosophers. They

44

do not endeavour to explain Creation, nor will they occupy themselves with revealing the mysteries which preceded the acts of Creation. Says the medieval exegete Nachmanides: "This is one of the mysteries of the Torah. If its author would have wanted to be better understood, he surely would have been more explicit. [But since he did not do so], we have no right to fathom what he covered with a veil."[7]

Jewish traditional exegesis does not entirely disregard some discrepancies between various passages of the present Creation account but tends to get around the problem by conceiving of the entire pericope as a developing tale: the overall presentation of cosmogony in chapter one (which critical scholars ascribe to P), leads to the fashioning of man in chapter two (which critical scholars ascribe to J), as a crowning piece of Creation.

But some discrepancies and the internal tension which surfaces in the account cannot be glossed over, as can be seen in the following examples. Himself perfect and omniscient, the Creator-God nevertheless could not prevent his work from going awry. He therefore destroys it (Genesis 6:5-8) and has to fashion a new universe. He is the sole and sovereign ruler of the cosmos, the only source of the laws by which it is governed and yet, after the Flood submits to his self-imposed restriction never again to destroy the work of his hands, he sets the rainbow in the skies as a memorial and a reminder both for himself and for mankind that the once-established order of Creation should never be disturbed again (Genesis 8:22 and 9:12-16). We may add here that midrashic Jewish tradition has it that the present world was established after God had destroyed a series of successive previous creations.[8]

A similar internal tension can be observed in the depiction of man. On the one hand, it is stressed that "God fashioned man of dust from the soil" (Genesis 2:7) and to "dust he will return" (Genesis 3:19). This idea is taken up in numerous passages in biblical literature; it became a prominent motif in post-biblical Jewish thought and, beyond that, is accepted in all civilizations that acknowledge the Hebrew Bible as a cornerstone of their culture. On the other hand, God appoints man as ruler of the universe, delegating to him authority over the entire Creation: "be fruitful, multiply, fill the earth and conquer it. Be masters of the fish of the sea, the birds of heaven and all living animals on the earth ... I give you all the seed-bearing plants that are upon the whole earth and all the trees with seed bearing fruit; this shall be your food" (Genesis 1:28-9). Man's mastery over Creation is further evinced by his giving "names to all the cattle, all the birds of heaven, and all the wild beasts" (Genesis 2:20), an act which clearly symbolizes his assumption of authority over all living creatures.

These discrepancies, which sometimes amount to contradictions, disturb the modern rationalistic Western mind but were accepted by Jewish thinkers with equanimity. As a matter of fact, we may discern here the imprint of a thought process which, unlike Hellenistic thought controlled by the "law of non-contradiction", acquiesces to the plurality inherent in human experience.

This phenomenon was discerned by Gershom Scholem in relation to the intellectual world of post-biblical Judaism. Modified and adjusted, his observations can be applied to biblical literature in general and to the Creation narrative in particular:

> It is precisely the wealth of contradictions, of differing views, which is encompassed and unqualifiedly affirmed by tradition. There were many possibilities of interpreting the *Torah*, and tradition claimed to comprise them all. It maintains the contradictory views with astounding seriousness and intrepidity, as if to say that one can never know whether a view at one time rejected may not one day become the cornerstone of an entirely new edifice.[9]

The three stages of Creation

Generally speaking, the biblical Creation traditions mirror a perception of three stages in the making of the universe. A similar conception underlies the creation myths of so-called pre-literate cultures, for example in the South Seas or in South America, as well as those preserved in literatures of the ancient Near East, in Egypt and in Mesopotamia: *theogony*, the creation or emanation of deities, precedes *cosmogony*, the fashioning of the universe, which for its part is succeeded by *anthropogony*, the creation of man. It is obvious that the notion of a pre-existent immanent God, which permeates biblical monotheism, ruled out any possibility of Israel's developing a theogony. The total and absolute rejection of any reflection on the origin of God is seen in the fact that even the aforementioned residues of pagan creation myths preserved in the Bible never pertain to theogony. The primordial deities are portrayed at a stage in which they are engaged in a struggle over the creation of the universe and man, and no thought is given to the question of how they themselves came into existence.

One is inclined to perceive in this absence of any discernible trace of theogony one other indication of the basic biblical orientation toward man and his place in the world. It appears that rather than being theocentric, the Hebrew Creation tradition is first and foremost anthropocentric, then ethnocentric. From here follows that in order to fathom the intrinsic meaning of the biblical Creation tradition, we must go beyond Genesis chapters 1 and 2 and bring under scrutiny also the ensuing block of texts (chapters 3-11) which precedes the narrowing of the focus on the history of the people of Israel, beginning with Abraham's exodus from his native land (Genesis 12:Iff.).

Viewed in this larger framework, the biblical account tells of two successive creations which exhibit manifest similarities. Both accounts emphasize the basic principle on which the universe is founded: the cosmos was created as an all-embracing organism consisting of diverse and differentiated natural phenomena, creatures and species, and should remain distinct forever. All mixed breeds are anathema. There is to be no crossing the lines which divide species, above all the borders which set apart animal from man and the human world from the divine sphere. This principle embodies a particularity characteristic of the biblical world of ideas. Mythological cosmogonies, entertained by ancient Near Eastern societies or current among pre-literate peoples, do not proclaim this total separation of beast and man, of man and deity. Quite the contrary. In such mythic tales, crossbreeds of many colours and shapes roam the scene: heroes and centaurs, demigods, nymphs and flying dragons, all serving as welcome objects for depiction and plastic representation.

The story of the primodial Creation (Genesis 1:1-6:12) comprehends cosmogony, leading up to anthropogony (Genesis 1:2),[10] then depicts the first *man's* fate, presenting to the reader what could be viewed as an incipient biblical anthropology (Genesis 3-6). In the account of the history of the first *men*, there surfaces a literary pattern which will recur in biblical literature: a father begetting three sons, the youngest of whom will surpass his brothers. After Adam's death, Abel's murder at the hands of his brother Cain and the ensuing disqualification of Cain, the last born Seth is destined to ensure the continuance of the human race. This same pattern surfaces in the post-Deluge account of the second Creation, which is the creation of the prehistoric world. Noah takes centre stage in the narratives of the destruction of the world by the Flood and its re-creation but, even in his lifetime, his two sons, Ham and Japhet, serve as a foil for the third, Shem. Shem is accorded ascendancy over his brothers (Genesis 9:10-27): he is a precursor of Abraham, on whose descendants and their fate biblical literature will focus. Both accounts culminate in reports of the destruction of the created world as punishment for the transgression of the human race against the fundamental principle of the absolute differentiation between God and man.

But against this background of similarities, some telling differences between the two tales emerge. The immediate cause for the annihilation of the primordial Creation is the cohabitation of the "daughters of men" with the "sons of God", which produced the "heroes of old" (Genesis 6:1-4), evidently semi-divine creatures. The reported intermingling of humans with celestial beings suggests an underlying quest of man for the attainment of divine status.

The prehistoric world is nearly destroyed for a similar reason. The tale of the Tower of Babel gives evidence to the attempt of depraved mankind to "reach heaven", i.e. to arrogate to itself divine status (compare Genesis 11:1-4 with Isaiah 14:13-14). But in this instance judgement is mitigated. The punishment meted out to the offenders consists of the dissolution of their "oneness", which had generated the hubris. They are scattered over the earth (Genesis 11:1-9). Their reproachable oneness dissolves into a plurality of peoples, countries and languages. Thus, the divinely established differentiation of the first Creation is reconstituted (Genesis 11:11-32), providing the backdrop for the ensuing particular history of the people of Israel.

Viewed from another angle, the comprehensive tradition complex of Genesis 1-11 can be subdivided into two components, one of which (Genesis 1-2) is determined by the concept of either creation *ex nihilo* or creation by giving form to pre-existing amorphous matter. In contradistinction, the other component, also consisting of two sub-units (Genesis 3:1-6:8 and 6:9-11:32), is characterized by the concept of emanation. The difference can be partly explained by the fact that in the primordial (first) Creation all plants and living beings were invested with the faculty to procreate, which ensured the continued existence of all creatures after the Deluge. The disastrous flood did not totally annihilate the universe. Nature was merely subjected to a temporary eclipse. When the waters receded, the peaks of the mountains emerged, to be followed by the treetops, until the earth, freed from the last sheets of water, was again revealed in the form it had been given in the primordial Creation (Genesis 8:1-14).

All living creatures were reduced to the barest minimum but, after the disaster had passed, this minimum allowed for a regeneration. According to one tradition, the animal world was cut back to one pair of every species (Genesis 6:19-20). According to another, seven pairs of all ritually clean animals were preserved and one pair of all ritually unclean animals. Similarly, mankind was reduced to one other "first couple" — Noah and his wife — replacing the primary "first couple" — Adam and Eve. Adam and Eve had been placed by God in the garden of Eden; Noah and his wife were saved from destruction by being put into the Ark. Adam and Eve became the forefathers of "all those who live" (Genesis 3:20) — "procreating" whereas God had "created". But biblical Hebrew uses one and the same vocable, *qnh* for describing these diverse manners of creation. Having given birth to her firstborn, Eve proudly proclaimed: "I have [pro-]created *[qanitt]* a man like YHWH" (Genesis 4:2). This proclamation echoes a statement in Deuteronomy 32:6, where it is said of God: "Is he not your father, your creator, *[qaneka]* he made you *[asafez]* and fashioned you?" (compare this with Proverbs 8:22-30). Procreation which, after the first Creation, was obviously considered an outstanding human achievement, notwithstanding the birth-pains which went with it as a divine punishment (Genesis 3:16), became commonplace in the post-Flood recreation of the world. The production of offspring by Noah and his wife is recorded as a simple matter of fact. The account moves from the plane of primordial history to the plane of prehistory, which serves as a backdrop for the ensuing presentation of history proper.

Creation terminology

The biblical text exhibits a bewildering variety of vocables pertaining to creation. Terminology signifying technical acts of Creation is freely combined with the vacabulary which connotes emanation: *asah* — make; *banah* — build; *yatsar* — fashion. All these terms apply equally to the Creator, God, and to man, his regent on earth. One other term that is used both in reference to God and man, *hivdil* — separate, will be referred to later in detail.

Two terms are reserved for the description of God's acts alone. One is *amar* (speak), which, as is well-known, has a much wider application in biblical literature, but in the context under review signifies the act of Creation by divine fiat. The other is *bara* which occurs forty-nine times in the Hebrew Bible, with God as the exclusive subject. No definite etymological derivation can be established for *bara*, nor has its equivalent been found so far in other Semitic languages.[11] It is probably the most significant vocable both in the basic biblical Creation complex in Genesis and wherever it occurs elsewhere in the Bible with reference to Creation. The exclusive association of *bara* with creation acts of the one Creator, God, is highlighted by the fact that this root is never used in the Bible in passages which contain terminological residues of ancient Near Eastern cosmogonies. Nor is it used to describe man's creative activities, with two notable exceptions: with the connotation of *cutting down* trees for the 'creation' of arable land (Joshua 17:15, 18); and with the connotation of *cutting up* men with swords (Ezekiel 23:47; Ezekiel 21:24b is unintelligible and therefore may be left out of our consideration). While the prevalent translation "create" is acceptable, there are grounds for viewing *bara* as a parallel to *hivdil*, like it, signifying Creation by differentiation.

The pivotal aspect of Creation

"The suggested technical connotation of the term *bara*, create by separation", colours the meaning of the more general term *sah* (make), which also signifies creation by separation.[12] A survey of the most prominent verbs in the biblical account of cosmogony lends substance to the proposition that "differentiation" is the pivotal aspect of Creation. To 'create' means to give peculiar character and specific form to the diverse phenomena which together constitute the universe. A glance at the unfolding stages in the biblical account of Creation proves the point.

The first major step in the process is the separation of heaven and earth (Genesis 1:1: *bara*). Then follows the separation of light from darkness, identified with day and night respectively (Genesis 1:4, 5 and 1:18). This sets the stage for the emergence of the earth as man knows it. Thereafter, the division of day and night with respect to heaven is achieved by God's fashioning *(asah)* the two great luminaries: the sun governing day and the moon governing night. The two together are set apart from the minor luminaries, the stars. Again, as with the differentiation between the (day)light and the darkness (of night) on earth, the distinction between the diverse heavenly bodies is indicated by *hivdil* (Genesis 1:14-18 and 4-5; Jeremiah 31:35; Psalm 136:5-9).

Once "night" has been separated from "day", a distinction is introduced into "day" itself. The Creator sets apart the seventh day of this and every week from the preceding six "work-days" and declares it to be a "holy day of rest" (Genesis 2:1-3). It should be pointed out that the root *qadosh*, by which the special character of the seventh day is singled out, *vayeqaddesh oto* (compare Exodus 20:8 with Deuteronomy 5:12), in biblical and later Jewish tradition can again signify separation. The principle of differentiation, applied to the luminaries in the upper spheres, is given further expression when heaven is perceived of as a flat sheet (*raqia*, Genesis 1:8), which divides the supracelestial from the infracelestial waters (1:7). This act of division is defined by *hivdil*.

Next, the dry land becomes earth and is segregated from the seas (*yamirri*) by God's gathering the terrestrial waters (*mayim*) in one mass or place (Genesis 1:9-10). This detachment of the seas from the dry land seems to reflect mythological imagery, as shown above: having vanquished his primordial foes, the creator deity puts Yam (the god of the sea) in fetters by setting the sands of the seashore as his eternal limits.

Now that the sea has been divided from the dry land, the earth (Genesis 1:10) can produce vegetation, plants and trees, again differentiated from the very beginning into their various and distinct kinds, *lemino* (1:11, 12). Parallel to that, by a divine fiat (*arnar*), the seas bring forth various kinds of creatures (Genesis 1:20, 21b). These evidently natural beings are distinguished from the originally mythological great *taninim*, whom God creates separately (Genesis 1:21a, *bard*). Like the seas which are teeming with various species of aquatic beings, *leminehem*, the heavens are populated by diverse kinds of winged creatures, *leminehu* (Genesis 1:20-21). The same pertains to earth, which is said to have produced "every kind of living creature: cattle, reptiles, and every kind of wild beast" (Genesis 1:24, 25). The recurring insistence upon diversity cannot be overlooked (compare 7:14).

Man is altogether distinct. God makes man (asah/bara) in his likeness or image (*betsalmenu kidmutenu*) (Genesis 1:26, 27) and therefore different from all other species of living creatures. Moreover, differentiation shows also in the very act of making man. Mankind appears on the scene in two separate sexes, male and female (Genesis 1:27): in one tradition, from the very outset; in another, in a two-stage development, the female being derived from the male (Genesis 2:21-3).[13] This latter notion of the separation of mankind into sexes cannot be reconciled with the former notion of man's being created in the image of God, since God is seen to be indivisible and sexless. While the anthropomorphic thrust of the vocabulary cannot be denied, the glaring internal contradiction can be only mitigated if in this context *tselem* and *demut* are not understood in the literal sense of physical likeness, but are given less tangible connotations. And indeed, when interpreted contextually, the likeness implied in the Hebrew terms *tselem* and *demut* appears to aim at the Creator's dominion over the universe, rather than at a visual perception of his "image". Such an understanding is achieved if we explain the relevant passages by having recourse to an 'inbuilt' means of interpretation. Frequently, an obscure or opaque phrase in one verse or in one part of a verse will be clarified by another part or another verse whose meaning is unequivocally clear. Applied to the texts under review, the crucial passages would read as follows:

> God said: "Let us make man, like us to assume mastery over the fish of the sea, the birds of heaven, the cattle, all the wild beasts and all the reptiles that crawl upon the earth." God created man in his likeness ... blessed him and said to him: "Be fruitful and potent, fill the earth and subdue it. Be master of the fish in the sea, the birds of heaven and all living animals on the earth" (Genesis 1:26-8).

Thus understood, the "likeness" of which the text speaks would not pertain to the physical image, but rather to the similarity of function. The mastery over the world accorded to man indeed reflects God's rule over the universe. However, being but a reflection of divine omnipotence, man's mastery amounts in fact to stewardship: he is called upon to preserve and to fashion, within limits, what God had singularly created *(bard)*. By stressing its derivative nature, the biblical tradition severely circumscribes man's power and actually denies him the right to subject Creation to fundamental changes. Man is doubly bound by God's promise, after the destructive flood, that Creation will not be affected any more by radical upheavals: "Never again will I strike down every living being as I have done. As long as earth lasts, sowing and reaping, cold and heat, summer and winter, day and night shall cease no more" (Genesis 8:21-2 and Jeremiah 33:20, 25-6).

From text to principle

These texts cannot be construed as a detailed blueprint for personal and societal behaviours but they offer principles which can be adapted to novel situations in which humans, individuals and societies, find themselves.

The appointment of man as "master of the universe", which is symbolized in his giving names to all living beings (Genesis 2:20), leads, almost unavoidably, to the emergence of human hubris, man's aspiration to achieve a status beyond what was accorded him in the divine plan. "When man began *(larov)* to assume mastery over the earth" (Genesis 6:1 and 1:28), he also began to mix with celestial beings; the "daughters of men" cohabited with the "sons of God" (Genesis 6:2). The Bible emphatically rejects this commingling of super-humans with humans. Although the episode does not pertain to Creation itself but rather is given as the reason for its undoing (Genesis 6:1-7), it should nevertheless be viewed and evaluated in the context of the basic motif of separation which permeates the Creation account. In the condemnation of the fusion of categories which the Creator had meant to be separate, we may discern a concomitant rejection of any positive attitude toward demigods, heroes and other beings, who blur the impenetrable border

51

between this the human world and the heavenly spheres. Such belief in the existence of intermediate beings found a prominent expression in ancient Near Eastern cultures in the self-aggrandizement and the popular veneration of royalty. The biblical repudiation of these offensive notions is highlighted in the prophecies of Isaiah against the King of Babylon (Isaiah 14) and of Ezekiel against the King of Tyre (Ezekiel 28) respectively. Both rulers aspired to divinity; each wanted to set up his throne next to, if not in place of, the throne of God (Isaiah 14:13-14; Ezekiel 28:2, 13-14). Both were smashed to earth by God and thus reduced to their proper position of human inferiority.

The biblical Creation tradition, especially the account in Genesis 1, reads like an ancient treatise which conceives of the universe as a whole, made up in orderly fashion of clearly defined categories. It resembles didactic wisdom literature which offers information in the form of onomastica, in which are enumerated diverse species and subdivisions of species of various phenomena observable in the universe. The Bible ascribes the composition of such rosters to King Solomon, whose wisdom is said to have surpassed that "of all the sons of the East and of Egypt ... he composed three thousand proverbs and his songs [of instruction] numbered 1005. He could talk about plants from the cedar in Lebanon to the hyssop, and he could talk of animals, and birds, and reptiles and fish" (1 Kings 5:9-13). The biblical creation account can therefore be viewed as an attempt on the part of ancient man to overcome taxonomic confusion and to grasp in an orderly fashion the bewildering number and variety of phenomena which confront him in his world, without blurring their differences. Indeed, "Genesis 1 personalizes the classification of the world." [14]

Equally, post-biblical Jewish tradition insists on keeping apart what was created differently. It has been surmised that this principle could explain the large number of injunctions against mixing species. [15] Biblical law proscribes the interweaving of wool and flax and the cross-breeding of different kinds of animals. Dietary laws forbid the consumption of creatures which exhibit characteristics of more than one basic species, such as aquatic mammals or insects which both fly and crawl. Applied to the human sphere, this principle underlies the interdiction of intermarriage between members of different ethnic and/or religious groups. The objection essentially evidences a positive intention to preserve distinctions and relations rooted in Creation — actually in the recreation of the universe after the Flood — rather than a negative, overbearing attitude towards outsiders.

There emerges in the Jewish tradition a structured universe in which each species, different and separate from others, is accorded its appropriate place in the divine economy. Particularity and an all-embracing universality are seen as complementary, rather than mutually exclusive. Judaism recognizes particularity not only as an undeniable principle of human existence but as divinely decreed. It confers a spiritual dimension upon actual particularity, such as is experienced in all life situations; it is a basic phenomenon of the human condition from the days of creation — anthropologically, ethnically, socially and politically. Particularity implies diversity of all beings and, therefore, also the separateness of man — under the unifying overlordship of the Creator who reigns supreme over all mankind. The underlying tenet could be defined with Jaques Maritain as: "distinguer pour unir". Judaism affirms the resulting diversity in the realm of the human spirit. It considers multiformity as a reality of human history — in the physical world as in the world of ideas and beliefs.

The blending of Creation with history

The taxonomic character of the biblical Creation account, apparent in the principle of categorization, can further be discerned in the presentation of the progressive socialization of man.

As already pointed out, the story begins with the defining of the relation of man to other species and to nature, in the wider sense of the word, by his being appointed as their master. Then we are translated to another plane. Man as an individual is depicted in the most basic interhuman relationships, primarily within the framework of the nuclear family: husband with wife (Genesis 2:22-4 and 3:6, 12, 16-17), sibling with sibling (Genesis 4:1-16). Thereafter, the canvas is enlarged. "The roll of Adam's descendants" or possibly "the account of man's origins" (Genesis 5:1-2) endeavours, in fact, to reveal the progress of "history" in the form of a series of interconnected genealogies. Such genealogies, based on the generation-cycle, the issue of a son from his father, may be viewed as an early attempt to capture the causal interdependence of events in their chronological sequence. At this stage, family relations, birth, marriage and procreation pertain no longer to the individual alone. They are rather a means for expressing relationships between social units. The story of 'first man' as a prototypical individual becomes the story of "first men", who are but personified collectivities (5:3-32).

The account of this progressive socialization is further refined by connecting man's basic occupations and crafts to the very beginnings of the world. Man starts out as a "food gatherer" in the "garden" provided for him by the Creator (Genesis 2:8-17). When expelled from the Garden as a punishment for his transgression, he becomes a "horticulturist", working the recalcitrant soil 'by the sweat of his brow' to extract from it his daily bread (Genesis 3:17-19). Further categories are introduced in the confrontation of Cain, "the agriculturalist", and his brother Abel, "the herdsman" (Genesis 4:2ff.). One of Cain's descendants, Jabal, removed from Cain by several generations and considered "the ancestor of the tent-dwellers and owners of livestock" (Genesis 4:20), obviously continues his forefather's occupational line. Jabal's half-brother, Tubal-Cain, is introduced as the progenitor of "all metalworkers in bronze or iron" (4:22), a technical trade which appears to have been closely affiliated with the growing of livestock. Jabal's brother, Jubal, represents the finer arts: "he was the ancestor of all who play the lyre and the flute" (4:22).

The crafts which are missing from that list are no less interesting than the occupations recorded as having arisen in the primordial stage. There is, for example no mention of a first fisherman or a first sailor. This accords with the fact that biblical writers considered seagoing highly dangerous, as can be seen, for example, in the Psalm of Jonah (Jonah 2). The imagery pertaining to the sea carries over notions of destruction and peril that go with the primordial deity Yam of ancient Semitic cosmology. Normally, seafaring was not an occupation in which the ancient Hebrews commonly engaged. When they did engage in it, the results were disastrous. This is demonstrated by the report on the attempted maritime enterprise of Jehoshaphat, King of Judah, which ended with his ships being wrecked at Etzion-Geber (1 Kings 22:49 and 2 Chronicles 20:37). Solomon's seafaring undertakings were successful because his men teamed up with the men of Hiram, King of Tyre, "sailors who knew the sea" (1 Kings 9:27 and 2 Chronicles 8:18). Thus, it would appear that the curtailed roster of trades in the cluster of genealogies pertaining to primordial times reflects the existential experience of the ancient Israelite writers.

Biblical tradition places the beginnings of Yahwism in the primordial age. Scripture states that in the days of Adam's grandson, Enosh, "the name of YHWH was first invoked".[16]

In the ensuing stage of man's development, set in the world recreated after the Flood, wider aspects of social organization come to the fore. The "table of nations" (Genesis 10) visualizes the emerging "peoples" in their mutual relations, each implanted in their "country". Thus, the diversity of ethnic entities and their attachment to particular geographical areas is recognized and affirmed. By being included among the cosmological "firsts", the ethnic and political compositeness of humanity is given an almost prescriptive authority. This conception of man's basic constitution, coloured by an Israelite ethno-centric bias, is reflected in the Song of Moses which declares: "When the Most High gave the nations [their] appointed lands, when he divided mankind, he fixed their boundaries according to the number of the sons of Israel" (Deuteronomy 32:8; see also Numbers 23:10).

It is worthy of mention that while the Bible registers the diversity of man in terms of ethnic, geographic and political particularity, there is no reference whatsoever to a differentiation by colour. Indeed, such a differentiation subsequently emerges in biblical records which pertain to historical actualities. This late emergence suggests that, in the biblical world of ideas, the differentiation of man by colour is considered secondary and in no way has the fundamental value which attaches to particularities that are considered to be rooted in the constitutive phase of the primordial aeon.

I tend to interpret similarly the absence of any reference to forms of socio-political organization in the biblical Creation account. Other ancient Near Eastern civilizations conceived of "kingship" as being part and parcel of cosmogony. From the very inception of the world, kings were known to have ruled in an orderly succession, amounting to what might be defined as dynasties. Lists of primeval kings were preserved in Sumerian and Babylonian texts. In other parts of the world, as for example on Madagascar and Tongareva, traditions concerning societal organization from the beginning are also couched in terms of royalty. This very primordiality conferred a measure of sanctity on monarchy and on the person of the king. In contradistinction, such an ideological dimension did not attach originally to kingship in Israel. Rather is the institution of monarchy presented as having arisen out of specific historical circumstances. It emerged at a time when the sporadic and diffuse rule of the Judges-Saviours could not stem the advance of the Philistines, whose much more efficient political organization was superior to that of Israel. It was only at a later stage that one tried to undergird the *de facto* advantages of dynastic royal rule by providing it with a *dejure*, or an ideonic, basis by emulating conceptual foundations of political structures which prevailed in surrounding nations. [17]

The recognition of the basically realistic view of the world which inspires the biblical tradition of Creation leads us back to some remarks made at the outset of this presentation about the blending of Creation with history. The acquiescence in the bewildering multiformity of natural phenomena, the dissimilarity of human beings and, above all, the acceptance of the diversity which marks human society seem to reveal a process which could be defined as "historicization of Creation". The Hebrew Bible tends to view Creation in historical terms and to conceive of history in imagery drawn from the Creation accounts. In his daily prayers, morning and evening, a Jew praises God "who alone effects mighty deeds, makes new phenomena ... master of wondrous acts who in his benevolence forever renews Creation day after day."

Shemaryahu Talmon

NOTES

[1] Rabbi Joshua ben Hananiah holds that the world was created in the month of Nissan in which Passover falls (b. Talmud Rosh Hashanah 10b-11a).

[2] F. M. Cross, *The Ancient Library of Qumran and Modern Biblical Studies* (rev. ed.) (Grand Rapids 1980).

[3] See S. Talmon, "The calendar reckoning of the sect from the Judaean Desert" in C. Rabin and Y. Yadin (eds.), *Scripta Hierosolymitana 4* (Jerusalem 1965), 176.

[4] See, for example, H. H. Rowley, *The Growth of the Old Testament* (New York 1963), 137; J. Vajda, *Introduction à la pensée juive du moyen âge* (Paris 1947), 12.

[5] See S. Talmon, *King, Cult, and Calendar in Ancient Israel* (Jerusalem 1986), 9-12.

[6] The Revised Standard Version gives it as 41:1-5 while the Jerusalem Bible gives it as 40: 20-4.

[7] See, for example, S. W. Baron, *A Social and Religious History of the Jews. Vol. 8: High Middle Ages, Philosophy and Science* (New York 1965), 87ff.; E. Dantinne, "Création et séparation" in Le Muséon (Louvain), no. 74, 1961, 450-1.

[8] See Genesis Rabba 3:7, 9; Qphelet Rabba 3:11 and Midrash Psalms 34.

[9] Gershom Scholem, *The Messianic Idea in Judaism and Other Essays on Jewish Spirituality* (New York 1971), 290.

[10] See R. Albertz, *Weltschöpfung und Menschenschöpfung: Untersucht beit Deutero-Jesaja* (Creation of the World and Creation of Man: An Essay on Deutero-Isaiah) (Stuttgart 1974).

[11] For a discussion of the issue see A. Angerstorfer, *Der Schöpfergott des Alten Testaments* (The Creator God of the Old Testament), Regensburger Studien zur Theologie, no. 20 (Frankfurt 1979).

[12] See Genesis 1:26, 27; 2:3, 4; compare 1:25 with 2:9; also compare other passages which echo Creation terminology with Isaiah 45:7 and Amos 4:13; see further Exodus 34:10 and Isaiah 41:20 and 48:7.

[13] This particular feature of sex differentiation was not mentioned in reference to any previously created living being. It applies to the animal world only in the 'second creation' tradition, featuring Noah and the Ark (Genesis 6:19-7:16).

[14] K. Burke, *The Rhetoric of Religion: Studies in Logology* (Los Angeles 1970), 201ff.

[15] See Mary Douglas, *Purity and Danger* (London 1966).

[16] This statement contradicts other texts which maintain that God did not make himself known by his name YHWH even to the patriarchs: 'To Abraham and Isaac and Jacob I appeared as El Shaddai; I did not make myself known to them by my name YHWH' (Exodus 6:3). The first revelation of this specific divine epithet is reserved for Moses, and from that time he has been invoked by this name for all generations to come (Exodus 3:13-15).

[17] See Talmon, *King, Cult, and Calendar*, 16-37.

Creation in African religion

Introduction

This paper consists of two parts. The first is a general survey of creation ideas in African religion. Here African religion is used in the singular, to refer to the traditional religious systems of African peoples which have, in the course of history, developed but without religious founders. Various definitions of African religion have been offered, but it is not our aim to discuss them here.[1] The second part gives a few creation texts which we might use for further discussion.

There is a lot of material on African religion. It is estimated that Africa (which in this paper includes Madagascar) has a total of 2,100 distinct languages and dialects, spoken by some 3,200 ethnic groups (peoples).[2] Statistics are not always easy to come by in Africa, and lower figures of both peoples and languages of Africa are found in many circles. Whatever the correct statistics may be, the material on 'creation in African religion' is embarrassingly enormous. Most of the peoples (tribes) have each several creation accounts, myths and concepts. These accounts have been handed down through the oral tradition, some through symbols and rituals. With only a few exceptions, African peoples did not have the art of writing. This has meant, among other things, that early accounts of creation have proliferated orally into several variations in course of time. There is no central authority for the source of information, as is the case with the Bible for example.

While mutual exchange of creation and other concepts has been going on all the time among neighbouring and even, through travel, among distant peoples, some of the creation concepts are radically different among neighbouring peoples or ethnic groups. We have, in any case, to receive and interpret the creation accounts and ideas within the wider framework of people's religious and philosophical world-views and practices. In a large number of cases, creation accounts have still not been recorded in writing and hence have not yet reached the world of scholars. In other, or perhaps most, cases, these creation ideas have not been carefully analysed by scholars from the peoples concerned.[3] The material on which this paper is based is taken at its face value, leaving much to be understood more deeply.

Creation myths

We have already indicated that the creation accounts are countless. The theme of creation is no doubt the most common in African mythology. Myths in this category deal not only with the creation or origin of things as such, but often focus on the creation of man and the necessary elements for his life. They address themselves to a basic question in man's understanding of himself and the world in which he lives: whence is the world? Whence is man in the world? In daily life the place of children, parents, clan and 'tribe' has been important for the survival and the exercise of human relationships (love, peace, care, conflict etc.). So, on a more cosmic plane, man relates himself to the world around him and beyond. Just as he is "born" (begotten, created), so he interprets the world as also having been created, begotten. But, since man cannot fathom the 'when' of the birth of the world, he employs the technique of the myth. Because the myth stretches the world beyond the horizon of time, myth and history generally merge. History at the other end becomes myth and myth at our end becomes history. With myth we can reach beyond history, we can present that which is a-historical and pre-historical. The myth is an extremely powerful means of communication.

God is the Creator of all things

In creation myths, God is invariably the central actor. Indeed, this is so much the case in African religion, that there is a concentration of names of God describing him (or her, since in many African languages there is no masculine-feminine dichotomy grammatically) as Creator. Thus, for example, for the Akan of Ghana God is, among other things: Onyame (the Supreme Being, God the Creator of all things), Nana (Grand Ancestor), Borebore (Excavator, Hewer, Creator, Originator, Carver, Architect), Odomankoma and Oboadee (Creator). He is for the Ibo of Nigeria, among other characteristics: Chineke (Creator), Chukwuokike and Onyeokike (the person who creates), Ezechitoke (the King that creates), Onye kelu enu kee ani (the person who created heaven and earth). To the Tiv of Nigeria God is known as Aondo Gba Tar (God, the Carpenter).[4] To the Bemba of Zambia he is Kashawaliko (he who was there before any other thing came into being or was born). To the Zulu of Azania he is simply Umvelinqangi (the one who created everything). Indeed, for many African languages and peoples, the word for God simply means Creator, Maker, Originator, such as Ruhanga for the Ankore and Ban-yoro peoples of Uganda; Katonda for the Baganda of Uganda; Ki-bumba for the Gwere and Basoga of Uganda; Kyumbi for the Pare of Tanzania; Rog for the Serer of Senegambia; or Mwari (the Great Weaver) for the Ndau of Zimbabwe. Many appellations and subsidiary names of God describe him as Moulder, Creator, Divider, Architect, Builder, Father/Mother, Grandfather/Grandmother, Parent, Originator, Designer, Arranger, Raiser- or Caller-up (into existence), Assigner and so on.[5] Many of the names attributing creation to God are used without any creation myths. This would probably mean that the idea of creation was so firmly associated with God over many generations that to think or talk about God became synonymous with creation. Conversely, to speculate about the origin of things led invariably to thinking and talking about God.

In this case, God is beyond the nature of himself being created. Creation may derive from him and indeed he is the ultimate cause of creation. But he himself is not created and not creatable. So we have names of God which describe his uncreatability. For example, to the Mende of Sierra Leone he is Leve (Supreme Creator, the one who is high or up); to the Akan of Ghana he is Tetekwaframoa (he who is there now as from ancient times); to the Yoruba of Nigeria he is Orise (the very source of being, Source-Being); to the Basa of Cameroon, he is Hilolombi (Ancestor of Days, the one who has been there from the beginning); to the Akamba of Kenya, he is Mumbi na Mwatuangi (the ultimate Maker and the Cleaver or Assigner of details); to the Ashanti of Ghana, he is Bore-Bore (the First, Creator of all things); to the Ganda of Uganda, he is Kazooba (he who has seen many, many moon-periods, the Everlasting One); to the Ila of Zambia, he is Namakungwe (Originator, he from whom all things came) and Mu-namazuba (he of the suns, the Everlasting One); and to the Ngombe of Zaire, he is Ebangala (the Beginner). [6]

These names and appellations of God in African religion show us clearly that the world in the comprehensive sense has its origin in and from God. God himself is beyond creation, since he is the author and sustainer of creation. Creation has its beginning in him; he cannot be attributed the feature of being created, and other attributes consistent with his being must be made about him.

Assistance in creation

In a considerable number of myths of creation, God uses or is helped (or served) by other beings, to carry out the original process of creation and the ordering of the world. These beings (or personified forces or objects of nature) are, however, subject to God; they play an assigned role, not the original role of creating the world. They tend to deal with the creation of man and the orderly system of human life. West African peoples, more than others elsewhere in Africa, incorporate a lot of these helpers or servants of God in the process of creation. These are usual spirit beings, some of which may hold very 'high offices' in the sight of God according to the creation myths. For example, in Yoruba (Nigeria) accounts of creation,

> what is now our earth was once a watery, marshy waste. Up above was the skyey heaven which was the abode of Olodumare [God] and the divinities with some other beings ... What moved Olodumare to think of creating the solid earth, no one knows. However, he conceived the idea and at once carried it into effect. He summoned Orisa-nla, the arch-divinity, to his presence and charged him with the duty ... Orisa-nla came down and did as he was told ... Orisa-nla was assigned another special job. He was made the "creator" of human physical features for the future ... to mould man's physical form from the dust of the earth. He thus became the sculptor-divinity. But the right

to give life Olodumare reserved to himself alone forever. The instruction given to Orisa-nla, therefore, was that when he had completed his own part in the creation of man, he should lock up the lifeless form in a room and leave the place. Olodumare would then come and give breath, thus completing the creation of the human being.[7]

In other creation myths, animals like the chameleon and the lizard, birds and insects like the praying mantis and the spider (which here is "insect"), and personified objects like the moon, the sun and stars, also play a role in assisting God. In any case, God is invisibly behind the creation process and we only see it taking place through secondary agents as though they had been "programmed" to play their role that way. The first few lines of the Fulani creation story which we provide in full in the second part of this paper, are a clear illustration of this "invisible" hand of God at work, creating:

At the beginning there was a huge drop of milk.

Then Doondari [God] came and he created the stone.

Then the stone created iron;

And iron created fire;

And fire created water;

And water created air.

Then Doondari descended the second time.

And he took the five elements

And shaped them into man ...

Some symbols of creation

A number of common symbols are found in connection with creation myths and concepts. Heaven and earth are seen as husband and wife, male and female, twins, parents of all created things. These are all symbols relating to life and its procreation. In a real sense they signify the continuing process of creation, the process of change, the proliferation of life. Creation did not happen and stop: it continues, through new shapes, new forms, mixing what is there in order to produce what is not there.

In all cases, God is associated with the heavens: he dwells there, in the highest of them (where several heavens may exist). However, in many myths it is said that originally the heavens and the earth were linked by a cord, a rope, a spider's web, a ladder or simply by joining each other at the horizon. In various ways, this linking was broken up; the heavens retreated — and God also withdrew from the earth. The earth remained below, as the dwelling-place of man and other earthly creatures. In some myths the blame is put on man; in others, it was through the act of some animals like the hyena which, being (always) hungry, could not resist taking a bite at the leather cord or ladder between the two. In others, a calamity occurred, which led to God's withdrawal from the earth and hence the severing of heaven from earth.

The symbol of original unity of heaven and earth (or their twin-ness) is a reminder of the importance of physical and spiritual realities, the link or fellowship between man and God. It speaks of the dependence of man (on earth) on God (in heaven), hence the role of religion to keep the (now) invisible link between man and God. Although the separation has (mythologically) taken place, God has not abandoned the earth (world, mankind). The heavens still let down the rain, water, the symbol of life on earth. God is the Giver of Rain, the Giver or Maker of Children, the one who thunders or roars so that all nations be struck with terror, as the Zulu people of Azania call him (uMabonga-kutuk-izizwe-zonke). God visits the earth daily, symbolically through the sun, for which he is called Cheptalil by the Nandi of Kenya (which means he who gleams or dazzles), or Asis (Sun) by the Kipsigis and Elgeyo of Kenya, or Ruwa (Sun) by the Chagga of Tanzania, and Wang Chieng' (Eye of the Sun) by the Luo of Kenya. These are clear indications that the symbolic separation is an attempt to explain the paradox of God's invisible being and at the same time his abiding presence in the world, among men. He is both far and near, he withdrew from the earth but yet he comes and dwells upon the earth: his presence is physically discernible through rain, thunder, sunshine, creating of new life, and so on. Men reach to him through prayers, sacrifices, offerings, invocations, songs and rituals. The calabash is another common symbol in creation accounts. Its round shape is like a miniature world, the uterus of birth. It is used as a waterpot, with water symbolizing life. It is also used as a rattle when hard seeds or pebbles are inserted into it. When cut open, it is used as a receptacle for food, drinks and other household objects. Also cut into two halves, these symbolize heaven and earth, the twin-ness of creation.

> In Dahomey [Benin] the universe is sometimes said to be a sphere like a round calabash, the horizon being where the upper and lower lips of a divided calabash meet. That is where the sky and sea mingle, in an ideal place inaccessible to man. The earth is thought to be flat, floating inside the larger sphere, as a small calabash may float in a big one. Within the sphere are waters, not only at the horizon but under the earth ... The sun, moon and stars move in the upper part of the calabash. The place of the dead is uncertain, some think that they are above the earth, and others that they are in the invisible part below the inhabited earth. When God created all things his first concern was to gather the earth together, fix the bounds of the waters, and join the calabash close. A divine snake coiled itself round the earth to bring it together and keep it firm. He carried God here and there, establishing order and by his essential movement sustaining all things. [8]

This is a rather unusual creation account, but it is one full of symbolic language, used by the Fon.

But the snake is a common creature (symbol) in creation accounts. In the case of the Fon of Benin mentioned above, it is narrated that "when the world was created, the snake gathered the earth together with its coils and gave men a place in which to live. It still sustains the world and its coils must not be loosened lest everything disintegrates. It is said that there are 3,500 snake coils above the earth and 3,500 below." [9] The Elgeyo of Kenya narrate in their creation myth, that "God sent to earth a man and a snake, with the instruction that the man was not to eat any food until God arrived. When the two reached the earth, the snake persuaded the man to eat before God's arrival. On discovering it, God punished the snake by compelling it to move on its stomach." [10]

The snake is a symbol of immortality or of rejuvenation, by virtue of its ability to shed off its skin and retain a new one from underneath. In art forms where the snake may have its tail in the mouth, that is a symbol of the endlessness of the world (circle).

The creation of man

Most of the creation accounts move from the creation of the universe (world in general) to that of man in particular. Indeed, some accounts do not even mention the creation of the world and concentrate only on that of man. In most cases, man is created last, when the rest of the world is ready for his habitation. He is generally created as husband and wife or in two pairs. Some myths say that God brought man down from the sky (heaven) to the earth, thus having created him in heaven. Others narrate that God used clay to mould men. This is one of the commonest myths, which is understandable since people use clay to make pots and other utensils, or for building, and children use it for making toys or human figures. Indeed, the word for God as Creator is often the same word which is used of a human potter.

Generally, the original state of the first man is depicted as having been paradisal. It was "one of happiness, childlike innocence, immortality, or the ability to rise again after dying. God provided man with the necessities of life." In some accounts, it is said that the first men lived in heaven with God; others say that God lived with them on earth, or that in any case there was an active link between God and man, heaven and earth. God was parent (father-mother) and mankind his children. In several accounts, the names of the first couple are given, as for example by the Gikuyu of Kenya (Gikuyu and Mum-bi); the Abaluyia (Bukusu) of Kenya (Mwambu and Sela); the Lugbara of Uganda (Gborogboro and Meme); the Herero of Namibia (Mukuru and Kamangarunga); and the Bambuti Pygmies of Zaire (Mupe and Uti). These names are a further indication that the first men were not just like other creatures: they were personally distinguished by being given names. This is to say that God gave them a personality — he named them, thereby putting a concrete imprint on them, a specific nature, dignity and character on human beings. No other parts of creation have personal names, apart from a few cases where a servant or an assistant of God is given a name. At the same time, the men (who have names in some cases) are given particular responsibilities, gifts, duties, privileges and skills or knowledge.

Creation accounts specifically concentrate on the creation of man and the life he first led, or was intended to lead. It is as if God's creation reached its summit or climax with the creation of man. In many accounts the creation of man comes at the very end of the process — which is depicted as having taken several days to complete (four, five, six), or in a few cases longer. Still, in many accounts no time-scale or duration is mentioned. The Shilluk of the Sudan, for example, narrate that God made man out of clay. Then "He gave man legs with which to walk and run; hands with which to plant grain; eyes with which to see that grain; and a mouth with which to eat it. Afterwards God gave him the tongue with which to sing and talk; and finally ears, so that he may enjoy the sound of music, of dance and of the talk of great men. Then God sent man out, a complete man." [12]

" Uncreation" or loss of original state

A large number of accounts more or less conclude creation with the loss of man's original state of bliss. This is pictured differently. It includes the coming of death into the world, the separation between heaven and earth and of God and man, the loss of free food supply, the coming of diseases, suffering and fights, the breaking of rules of conduct among people, the coming of the curse upon man and the loss of certain original knowledge or abilities. All this amounted to 'uncreation' coming upon an otherwise glorious creation. In some cases the man was reponsible for the new state; in other cases it was brought about by other creatures (spiritual or animal). The worst loss was that of the primal gifts of immortality, rejuvenation and resurrection. [13]

However, God did not leave man to perish without his help. Contact with God could continue, though the separation had become firm. Man could reach God through prayer, ritual, sacrifice, offerings, special religious functionaries, and symbolically upon dying. God provided man with the means of survival. Through procreation man can still keep death at bay, and in some sense the departed continues to live through his offspring. Furthermore, death does not annihilate the person. Instead, there is a continuation of life beyond, the next life being pictured often as a carbon copy of the present but continuing more or less indefinitely in the spirit world. All this in a sense means that creation has been disrupted by "uncreation" (but on a scale almost confined to man, though with consequences upon the rest of creation). God in his great power and wisdom has, however, not let "uncreation" have the final word: he has provided ways for a form of "re-creation" to supersede "uncreation", so that the process of creation is still very much at work, God is still in control and man is, on a smaller scale, a participant in God's work of "re-creation".

Creation without end

God is thus not only Creator and Moulder of the world: he is also its Sustainer and Upholder, so that it does not (and cannot) disintegrate.

Indeed, in African cosmology, there is no end of the world, no end of time. There are only myths of the beginning of creation. There are, for all practical purposes, no myths of the end of creation. Creation begins from God — whatever the different myths may say. But people do not imagine that this creation could come to an end, since such an end would have to involve God himself, but for him there is no end. Were creation to come to an end, it would leave God still in existence. But what would be the purpose of his being without creation, alone? As it is, creation was purposed by God and, with his word, summoned into being. No purpose would be served were the creation to come to an end. African religion does not address itself to this end of the scale. Instead, African religion firmly and variously describes God as "everlasting", "he who is there now as from ancient times" (Tetekwafra-mua, by the Akan of Ghana), "Giver of light or sun" (Amowia, also by the Akan), "he who makes all things multiply, Multiplier" (Nalusa-ndulula, by the Bemba of Zambia), "he who has seen many, many moon-periods, the Everlasting One' (Kazooba, by the Ganda of Uganda), "he of the suns, the Everlasting One" (Munamazuba, by the Ila of Zambia), and so on. These qualities, concepts and attributes of God are intricately linked to his creation and "re-creation". His very being upholds that which he has caused to come into existence. Where part or parts of that creation come to some kind of end, this is to be understood within the purposes of God, also when those purposes lie hidden in the wisdom of God. African religion has concerned itself more with what has been and is than what might not be — with creation and the God who authored it, sustains it and is involved in it.

Texts on creation in African religion

The Fulani creation story (Mali, Senegal etc.)

At the beginning there was a huge drop of milk.
Then Doondari [God] came and created the stone.
Then the stone created iron;
And iron created fire;
And fire created water;
And water created air.
Then Doondari descended the second time.
And he took the five elements
And he shaped them into man.
But man was proud.
Then Doondari created blindness, and blindness defeated man.
But when blindness became too proud,
Doondari created sleep, and sleep defeated blindness;
But when sleep became too proud,
Doondari created worry, and worry defeated sleep;

But when worry became too proud,
Doondari created death, and death defeated worry.
But when death became too proud,
Doondari descended for the third time,
And he came as Gueno, the eternal one,
And Gueno defeated death. [14]

Bam butt Pygmies (Zaire) — a summary

They tell that God made the body of the first man by kneading, and
then "covered him with a skin and poured blood into his lifeless body.
Then the first man breathed and lived, and God whispered softly in his
ear, 'You will beget children who will live in the forest' ". This man was
called Baatsi. [15]

Pygmies (Zaire) : hymn or creed

In the beginning was God [Kmvoum]
Today is God,
Tomorrow will be God.
Who can make an image of God?
He has no body.
He is a word which comes out of your mouth.
That word! It is no more,
It is past, and still it lives!
So is God. [16]

Dinka (Sudan)

In the time when God created all things,
He created the sun.
And the sun is born and dies and comes again.
He created the moon,
And the moon is born and dies and comes again.
He created the stars,
And the stars are born and die and come again.
He created man,
And man is born and dies and comes not again. [17]

The Mende creation story (Sierra Leone)

Ngewo, before He was called Ngewo, was once a very big spirit who lived in
a cave. He was so powerful that all He said would be done, took place. One
day He said, "I have all this power, why don't I use it? I have lived alone for
a long time with no one to talk to and no one to play with." Then He went to
the entrance of the cave and said, "I want all kinds of animals to live with Me
in this cave." So the animals came in pairs. Then He shut the door. After a
while, He called them all together and gave them the laws (rules) of the cave.
He said, "I will give you anything you want, food, and everything else, but
you must not touch My own food." Then the Spirit looked round about and
said, "This cave is too small." So He turned Himself around and the cave
became very, very big. The animals were now very happy, because they had
plenty of room to find food. All they had to do was eat. The Spirit, too, was

happy — He had neighbours to talk to and play with. The Spirit was so big that all the animals could not move even one of His legs. But the Spirit was very strict about the due observance of His laws (rules). One day, one of the animals came to greet the Spirit. As it approached, it smelled some sweet-smelling food. It saw the food and took some and ate it. Immediately it found itself in front of the Spirit. The Spirit said, "What brought you here? You have violated my law." The Spirit then threw the animal from the cave and said, "You! From now on, your name is cow." Later, another animal ate the food, and again the Spirit threw it out of the cave, saying, "You! From now on, your name is monkey." At last all the animals were thrown out of the cave. Some of the animals the Spirit called "man". That is how animals got their names. All the animals and men are still wandering around the world looking for this sweet-smelling food! The Spirit is now called Ngewo. He has now gone up far above men, where He is sitting, watching to see who will eat His food. Men and animals are now removed from Ngewo. The removal presumably means the loss of immortality which is His attribute. [18]

The Vugusu (Kenya) creation story: a summary

The Bukusu (sometimes spelt Vugusu) are a community which is one of the groups of communities collectively called the Luyia of Western Kenya. Their myths about the origin of the universe are closely connected with their belief in a Supreme God, who is called Wele or Nyasaye. They believe in this Supreme God as the Creator or Maker of the universe, and this belief is established in their traditional prayers and religious myths. However, the description of the exact method which Wele used in the creation of the universe varies. Whereas some of the Bukusu say that he created the whole universe in one moment, like lightning, others say he did so in one day, and yet others say that he created the universe in stages. Here is one interesting myth told by some of those Bukusu who believe that the universe was created in stages. The universe was created by Wele Khakaba, "the one who gives or grants all things". Wele Khakaba created the universe all alone, and he did so in two days. To begin with he created his own place, in which he could stay. That is heaven. Having created his own home, he went on to make all other things in the universe. He prevented heaven from falling by making pillars all around it. It is not known how Wele Khakaba created heaven. It is also not known of what heaven is made.

After creating heaven and supporting it on pillars, Wele Khakaba created two assistants, Mukhove and Murumwa. Heaven was always bright, because it was the house of this Supreme God and his assistants.

Wele Khakaba then created Moon, followed by a younger brother Sun. Moon shone more brightly than Sun in the beginning. Sun became jealous of Moon and attacked him. When they fought Moon won, and Sun begged for mercy. Moon forgave his younger brother and decided not to destroy him. However, Sun attacked again, and this time Moon was defeated. Moon was thrown down and covered with mud to prevent him from shining brightly.

During this second fight, Wele Khakaba, the creator arrived. He stopped the fight. He punished Moon for pitying and forgiving Sun during the first fight. The punishment was that Moon would not shine brightly any more. Sun would shine during the day on kings, leaders, and all other things, both good and bad. Moon, on the other hand, would shine only for thieves and witches at night.

Following the creation of Sun and Moon, Wele Khakaba made a big cock, which brings lightning and thunder. The cock has reddish feathers, and lives among the clouds. Lightning is seen whenever the cock shakes its wings and thunder is heard whenever the cock crows.

Stars to assist Sun and Moon were created next. Two were created first: one for the east, which shines before dawn; and one for the west, which shines after sunset. Wele Khakaba then decided to put something in the clouds. Rain was created, and this was to be the source of water. To stop rain from falling when it was not needed, two rainbows were created — one male and the other female. The male one was narrow, but the female one was wider. The male one is unable to stop rain, but the female one can. In order to prevent rain, the male rainbow appears and is followed by the female one, which prevents the rain from falling.

Air was created next. This included the cold air which forms hailstones.

Wele Khakaba had now made his dwelling place, heaven, his assistants and everything else in heaven including the sun, the moon, stars, clouds, rain, rainbows, lightning and thunder. He then wondered where his two assistants would do their work. He therefore decided to make a workshop for them. This workshop is the earth. He did this in a mysterious way which is not known. In the earth he provided mountains, valleys and plains. [19]

John S. Mbiti

NOTES

[1] Practically all the books that treat the subject of African religion, make and elaborate on the definition of African religion(s). Among others see: J. Omosade Awolalu and P. Adelumo Dopamu, *West African Traditional Religion* (Ibadan 1979); E. Bolaji Idowu, *African Traditional Religion: A Definition* (London 1973); John S. Mbiti, *African Religions and Philosophy* (London 1969; New York 1970); Kofi Asare Opoku, *West African Traditional Religion* (London 1978); E. G. Parrinder, *African Traditional Religion* (London 1962) David Westerlund, *African Religon in African Scholarship* (Stockholm 1985).

[2] David B. Barrett, 'The spread of the Bible and the growth of the Church in Africa' in *United Bible Societies: Bulletin* (Stuttgart), no. 128/9, third/fourth quarter 1982, actually published 1984, 5-18. These are the latest and most reliable figures on African languages and peoples.

[3] The main work done on African creation myths is that of the German scholar Hermann Baumann, *Schöpfung und Urzeit des Menschen im Mythus der afrikanischen Völker* (The Creation Story and the Beginning of Mankind in the Myths of the African Peoples) (second ed.) (Berlin 1964). One general study by an African is that of Obiakoizu A. Iloanusi, *Myths of the Creation of Man and the Origin of Death in Africa* (Frankfurt 1984). There is also the general work of the English scholar Geoffrey Parrinder, *African Mythology* (London 1967).

[4] Opoku, 14-18, 25.

[5] John S. Mbiti, *Concepts of God in Africa* (London 1970), with an appendix of names of God in Africa, 326-36.

[6] *Ibid.*, see also Opoku.

[7] E. Bolaji Idowu, *Olodumare: God in Yoruba Belief* (London 1962), 18-21.

[8] Geoffrey Parrinder, *African Mythology* (London 1967), 22.

[9] *Ibid.*

[10] Mbiti, *Concepts of God*, 103.

[11] Baumann's book is devoted to this theme; so also, but on a much smaller and more general scale, is that of Iloanusi.

[12] Mbiti, *Concepts of God*, 161ff.

[13] See further details in Ulli Beier (ed.), *The Origin of Life and Death* (London 1966); H. Abrahamsson, *The Origin of Death* (Uppsala, 1951); also Baumann, Iloanosi, and Mbiti, *Concepts of God*.

[14] Beier, If.; Wole Soyinka (ed.), *Poems of Black Africa* (London 1975), 57f.

[15] P. Schebesta, *Revisiting my Pygmy Hosts* (London 1936), English translation, 179f. Schebesta comments categorically, that when he heard this story 'any biblical influence on the Pygmies was out of the question'.

[16] T. C. Young, *Contemporary Ancestors* (London 1940), 146. He does not specify which Pygmy people he cites.

[17] John S. Mbiti, *The Prayers of African Religion* (London 1975; New York 1976), 143.

[18] Opoku, 19f., from W. T. Harris and H. Sawyerr, *The Springs of Mende Belief and Conduct* (Freetown 1968), 8f.

[19] Jesse Mugambi and Nicodemus Kirima, *The African Religious Heritage* (Nairobi 1976), 1-3. This is a summary from Gunther Wagner, T*he Bantu of North Kavirondo*, vol. 1 (Oxford 1949), 167-75.

Johannesburg 1995

The story of Jews and Christians meeting in Africa

In June 1976 fifteen thousand schoolchildren gathered in Soweto to protest the government's ruling that half of all classes in secondary schools must be taught in Afrikaans. A detachment of police confronted the schoolchildren and without warning, opened fire. Among the many victims was thirteen-year-old Hector Pieterson.

Almost 20 years later Christians from several countries in Africa and Jews from different countries throughout the world gathered to read Psalms and pray at the monument erected to the memory of Hector Pieterson and all the other martyrs in apartheid South Africa. For a Jewish-Christian dialogue this was an unusual event. Jewish-Christian dialogue is an occurrence mostly engaging Jews and Christians in Europe and in North America. History has made it so. Europe is still scarred from the Shoah and survivors in Europe and in North America have not forgotten. Christians and Jews meet in memory. There is today hardly any official Jewish-Christian dialogue on the European continent that does not include a visit to memorials of the Shoah, paying tribute to those who were annihilated. Jews and Christians in Europe meet in the silence of Auschwitz, the Warsaw ghetto and Theresienstadt. In North America there are museums dedicated to the eternal memory of the victims of the Shoah. Christians bow down in silent prayer and contemplate the fact that the Shoah was enacted on the Christian continent par excellence. Jewish participants in the dialogue are victims or survivors of the unspeakable.

The moment of silence and prayer at the memorial of Hector Pieterson in Soweto in June 1995 was thus different from similar occasions in Jewish-Christian dialogue. Here Jews and African Christians were gathered, not in front of a memorial to Jewish victims but black African schoolchildren, men and women. And although a memorial to the victims of apartheid, it surpasses its own context to symbolise also the stories of many peoples of Africa, afflicted by the exploitation and subjugation of colonialism. Colonialism has left indelible marks on all of Africa. The social Darwinism of colonialism and in its tow, mission societies, looked upon the African peoples as incapable of managing their own affairs, thus justifying the white exploitation of their resources. Missionaries viewed Africans as having no valid religious insights at all. In some way therefore the memorial in Soweto personifies the plight of the whole of Africa and the reading of scripture and prayer became that day a common celebration of acquired freedom for the people of South Africa and an expression of solidarity with all the peoples of Africa.

African Christian participants came from Benin, Botswana, Cameroon, Eritrea, Ghana, Kenya, Mozambique, Nigeria and South Africa to meet with Jewish representatives from Israel, South Africa, Switzerland, United Kingdom, USA and Zimbabwe in a consultation, sponsored by the World Council of Churches (WCC) and the International Jewish Committee on Inter-religious Consultations (IJCIC). It was said many times during the consultation that the world-view of the traditional rural African is close to a Jewish world-view, particularly as it is expressed in the Old Testament. Africans reading the Old Testament in its own right find similarities with their own life and culture: the role of the ancestor in the family and the community, the clear definition of family as extended family, the nomadic, cattle and sheep farmers, the sacrifices at times of birth, wedding, funeral and other indigenous ceremonies, the hand-washing ceremonies and the rite of circumcision. Also the question of polygamy as a necessary system to handle difficult economic conditions is referred to as endorsed by the Old Testament, albeit that the most common form of marriage in ancient Israel was monogamous.

There is since many years an ongoing attempt to recover the African traditions in what was once lost through conversion to a Christianity in Western garb. Reading of the Old Testament with African eyes contributed in many ways to a strengthening of African traditions and thinking. The question has for some time been raised among African theologians whether the African needs to be Christianised or should it rather be that the Christian faith needs to be Africanised. It is particularly in the so-called African instituted churches that an Africanisation of Christianity has seen its day. The Old Testament has here a role to play and not only as a typology for the New Testament. The biblical stories regarding the bondage of Israel have become a paradigm for their circumstances. The importance of dreams, visions and trances as media of the revelation of God are stressed as in the Bible. Old Testament pronouncements regarding rituals, taboos and regulations are of interest. Customs and institutions in Africa have their counterparts in the Old Testament: sacrifice, prophetism, the theology of nature, death and the hereafter. The Old Testament is perceived as a kindred spirit. Religion pervades life.

The theme of the consultation "Family — Community — Tradition" summarised many of these similarities and focused on the backbone of both the traditional African and Jewish communities. In both the African and Jewish traditions the family plays a crucial role in the presentation and transmission of moral and social values. The African tradition resonated in the telling of the midrashic legend Tanhuma Vayigash: "When God was about to give the Torah to Israel, he asked for guarantors. The children of Israel offered the Patriarchs and then offered the prophets. God didn't accept any of them as adequate guarantors. But when the children of Israel offered their children as guarantors, God accepted them and gave the Torah." Jewish life is guaranteed by the children. Continuity depends on the future and not the past.

Rapid social changes have in various ways had a traumatising effect on the family, causing destabilisation and raising fears about its survival. In Africa urbanisation is a threat to the family. The ancestral village, which manifests and expresses the extended family in its various aspects, is home. The city is not. It is exile. The consultation considered ways by which family life could be strengthened to counteract the encroachment of materialism, consumerism and hedonism, and to guard against the negative features of technology, urbanisation and media. The failure of the present culture, which wants to be a global culture, focuses on and demands too little of the individual. There is no correlation of rights and obligations. This world civilization promises comforts in abundance but requires very little in return. It is essentially a "yes" education; there is little training in the art of saying "no" to oneself.

In a culture, which is above all a culture of individualism, community is endangered. The criterion of individualism has become freedom, but a freedom that is not community-oriented but understood to provide first of all self-centred autonomy and independence. The words engraved on the Liberty Bell in Philadelphia, USA illustrate this truncated freedom. While proudly announcing liberty and freedom to all bereaved, using the words from Leviticus 25,10: "And you shall proclaim liberty throughout the land to all its inhabitants", there is no mention of the second part of the verse, which is the consequence of liberty: the ethical responsibility towards society, "It shall be a jubilee for you: you shall return, every one of you, to your property and every one of you to your family."

Our days witness a disintegration of societal values and a lack of a vision of cohesion. We lose increasingly the ability to give meaning to history. Only the moment seems to be of moment and "we can't go home again". There is little expectation of how to make sense of the past. "The past is a bucket of ashes", says Robert Frost. There is almost an aversion to tradition.

Africans and Jews identify with a living tradition as the fibre of their respective society. Thought-provoking African proverbs, similar to many of the proverbs of the Bible, regard tradition as a guiding principle for the present and the future. Such proverbs see the old generation as the living tradition, as the key to the present and the future. "He who does not have an old person in the home must be pitied" and "Everybody has been a child before, but not everyone has been an old man before." The Jewish mystic of the early 18th century Baal Shem-Tov echoed the same, saying that remembrance is the beginning of redemption. Tradition is not a meaningless burden to be carried along, something which has lost sense and significance and which now has to be brought along for its own sake. Contrary to widely held views, tradition, properly interpreted and implemented, is needed in any process of development and progress.

But tradition cannot be had except by great labour. Tradition has to interact with our today. We are not to live in the past but the past is to live in us. A change of mind is necessary, taking seriously the wisdom of the African proverb which says that "you better come out of your house before you have the right to say that your mother's soup is the best."

In a certain sense, Jews and Africans have experienced a common history, the history of the denigrated, of having had to carry the yoke of exclusion and exploitation. Nowhere is this more apparent than in South Africa, recently emerging out of the evil of apartheid. One session during the consultation dealt with the effects of apartheid on family and community. Comparisons between the Shoah and apartheid could not be avoided. How does one deal with the past? How does one live in the present? Can one forgive? Forget? Someone said in a passionate voice: "Nelson Mandela has forgiven the persecutors... (but he) has no moral mandate to pardon crimes and persecution perpetrated by the apartheid regime other than those committed against his own person, in the same way that Jews have no power of attorney to forgive those who murdered their six million brothers and sisters. (Mandela) has willy-nilly created a moral dilemma in this country. But there was also the powerful voice of reconciliation, moving and stirring. In order to heal the wounds of the past, the conflicts of the present and the uncertainties of the future, a profound change in minds and hearts is necessary. "The biggest challenge to South Africa is how to change the hearts of people. We have to humanise our dehumanised people — both black and white. We have to revive black consciousness, white consciousness and national consciousness. We need to revive ubuntu. It is ubuntu to love and care for others. It is ubuntu to act kindly to others. It is ubuntu to be hospitable. It is ubuntu to be just and fair. It is ubuntu to be compassionate. It is ubuntu to assist those in distress. It is ubuntu to be truthful and honest. It is ubuntu to have good morals. A country which practises ubuntu is the closest thing on earth to the kingdom of God. Forgiveness must not be cheap and reconciliation cannot be glossed over. There is in South Africa today a spirited energy coming out of the people in their decision to engage in a collective reconciliation.

The consultation of African Christians and Jews contributed to many mutual discoveries, which will contribute to strengthened relations between Jews and Christians worldwide. Meeting in South Africa added another dimension to this relationship, the example of a country and people determined to heal the sore wounds of apartheid. In their own particular situations Jews and Christians may learn from this intentional process of reconciliation.

Hans Ucko

Family life in present times: fears and hopes

The family is the basic institution of society worldwide. One of the characteristics of African society is its diversity in terms of ethnic groupings, languages and customs. Some African peoples have traditionally been cultivators, others nomadic pastoralists, others hunters and gatherers and still others have combined elements of pastoralism, hunting and cultivation. Some communities in Africa are matriarchal and matrilineal while the majority are patriarchal and patrilineal. Politically some ethnic groups have been kingdoms, others have practiced some form of feudalism and still others have governed themselves on the committee principle. In their cosmologies some African communities have recognised several divinities both male and female, others only one.

In this diversity, however, the family has been the most important feature of the African society and indeed its very foundation. Some of the most elaborate socio-religio-cultural rituals and ceremonies have been motivated by the desire to establish family units on a permanent footing and to maintain their well-being. Traditionally therefore marriage negotiations and wedding ceremonies have been elaborate and have incorporated deep religious thought and symbolism.[1] Many religious ceremonies and much of the education of the youth were traditionally centred in the home. The home was the focus of life, being the nerve centre of procreation, renewal of generations, and physical sustenance of life from the cooking pot and the granary.[2]

This paper is on family life today. Even to the casual observer the family in contemporary African society has many strengths and many weaknesses. It is precariously balancing both to the point of being something of a contradiction. Perhaps because social change is rapid but culture dies hard African society is able to accommodate many contradictions. Family sense is strong in Africa and yet that is where some of the deepest hurts are being felt.[3] Many tears are rolling down in our communities and yet some of the most spontaneous laughter is heard in the same communities. Some people come to Africa to plunder but a number of Africans in the diaspora return to enjoy home life. Some of the most meaningful occasions in Africa today are weddings and family gatherings. But funerals have a way of affirming the bond that exists in kinship and in friendship. In this sense some of the most rewarding occasions are funerals that occur in the homelands and however educated and urbanized some Africans are "home" is the place of final rest.[4]

These are some of the realities of contemporary African society that make the sub-title of this paper apt. There is much consternation about the future of the family in Africa because there is much to cause despair. But there are strong seeds buried in the debris. The rest of this paper attempts to describe the debris and to identify the seeds. Faith in the living God and testimony of God's intervention in the affairs of humankind to rescue and restore prompts me to conclude from the outset that fears may abound but hope is there because, as my people say, Ngai ndaninukagia mbeu (God does not annihilate seed). Faith should prompt action and I am persuaded that action to salvage what is good in family life is a priority in our time.

Threats to family life in Africa

Many factors combine to undermine the family institution today in Africa. The recent genocide in Rwanda and the relatively similar situations elsewhere in Africa pose real doubts about the future of the family in Africa. Violations of family life have occurred under the slave trade when thousands of able-bodied sons and daughters were frog-marched to the west coast and the east coast and were displaced forever. Africa under European colonial rule experienced further violence against the family with the conscriptions for labour in white settler farms and as carrier corps (during the First World War in parts of East Africa).[5]

Both oral and written history tend to blunt the reality of the toll against families when they generalize ("many dead" or "lost") or when they give statistics. However, in the same way that every bird in the air is unique and therefore known to its Creator, every dead, missing, imprisoned or lost member of a family leaves a wound in the family. And so the family life in Africa continues to suffer from the inter-tribal wars of yesterday, the ethnic clashes of today which utilize modern deadly weapons. Natural calamities play their part in devastating families through drought and famine and even floods.

It is not possible to do justice to the issue of threats to the family in Africa. There is an interplay of many factors and the best one can do is to illustrate by selecting certain realities that are more immediate and contemporary. The list is alarming when we consider the many socio-political, economic, cultural and ideological factors that militate against family life in Africa. Suffice it to mention some of them and then describe briefly some of them. The threats include wars and political unrest, breakdown of morality, poverty, natural calamities such as drought, modernity and shifting concepts about the family, breakdown of marriages, domestic violence, and the AIDS epidemic.

Breakdown of morality

Probably because many factors responsible for the rapid social change in Africa are not neatly definable, there is much bewilderment regarding the moral decadence so evident in African society today. The devastating effect of rapid religio-socio-cultural change needs to be recognised. To illustrate from one case study, a few statements by some of the agents of change among the Gikuyu of Central Kenya are appropriate. Writing in 1923 to celebrate twenty-five years of missionary activities of the Church of Scotland Mission, A.R. Barlow has this to say:

> Civilisation has come upon them with a rush since the first white men came amongst them. Many influences are now extended upon them which are changing their ideas and their manner of life for good and for evil... [6]

C. Cagnolo similarly looks at the Gikuyu after thirty years of "civilising" and is impressed by the progress,

> a good number of families, Christian or merely emancipated from barbarous customs, have adopted a standard of living with lodgings, diet and manner which border on the civilized. [7]

However, Cagnolo is alarmed by this headlong progress with the "startling suddenness" which strips the Gikuyu of their old beliefs which ruled their actions and renders them devoid of firm moral foundation. [8] By 1938 J. Kenyatta was expressing the Gikuyu people's lamentation that they were "no more where they used to be" and that, "All is confusion" [9] This aspect of morality change was regrettable:

> Religious rites and hallowed traditions are no longer observed by the whole community. Moral rules are broken with impunity, for in place of unified tribal morality there is now ...a welter of disturbing influences, rules and sanctions, whose net result is only that a Gikuyu does not know what he may or may not, ought or ought not, to do or believe, but which leaves him with no doubt at all about having broken the original morality of his people. [10]

On his part, H.E. Lambert, a colonial administrator states in his 1942 Annual Report on one of the Gikuyu administrative districts:

> Individualism is the most obvious political trend of the modern Kikuyu, and it has developed... with such rapidity that it constitutes the most serious threat to the structure of a society based not long ago on its very anti-thesis. [11]

Lambert concedes that Europeans have a duty to help the African return to "some sort of social stability" since

> it was our own infringement of his social system which removed him from the position of equilibrium he had achieved for himself before our advent. [12]

To complete this case study a relatively recent field enquiry solicited some reactions of a cross-section of Gikuyu about morality in the contemporary period. Below are some of the responses. [13]

A retired Church of Scotland Mission elder:

> Gikuyu laws, customs and traditions have been erased... Righteousness is gone. The righteous parent is dying sooner than later from grief. When a man steps out of his homestead he sees things he does not want to see.

Among the sights that dishearten the older generation are the increasing number of staggering drunkards, unmarried young girls who are pregnant and loitering youths in towns and rural shopping centres.

All these strike old people as both unconcerned about their plight and disdainful of the "ignorant" old people. In this connection another old man confesses,

> These days things have come to us in a very bad way... I see some things and experience bad nausea...

A female product ot Christian missionary education and evangelization has this to say:

> When missionaries taught us things of God and about the way to live they wanted chastity to prevail. What went wrong puzzles me. It puzzles me because they taught chastity...

She offers some explanation that what has come to the people is a phenomenon called, in her nation tongue, *Kiiriu* (modernism), which she confesses is difficult to decipher. All she is sure of is that the effect of modernity is that people behave contrary to their will. A retired minister of the church (a denomination of mission Christianity) offers a similar explanation and says that what has come is "civilisation". But he cannot help being cynical about the acquired civilisation as he comments on the prevailing lack of integrity:

> Yet a civilised man will deceive his wife, a civilised man will deceive his mother. Why does a full grown man tell lies?...Let a husband speak the truth to his wife.

The senior generation fear that the trend of things is leading to a situation in the future when persons who should be family members will have no mutual commitment, when home will be irrelevant and when children will belong to that nebulous entity called the government or state.

In this case study both the middle-aged and the youth sectors hold remarkably similar sentiments. The middle-aged people lament about their failure to control children and the youth complain about lack of example from the older members of the society.

The very fact that both the senior and the younger members of society agree that morality has broken down to the detriment of the family, indicates that there is something hopeful. Africa needs individuals and organised groups to work on the issue of moral bankruptcy. People are still teachable and every newborn is potential material for moral integrity or wretchedness. Teaching aimed at imparting moral integrity has never been a definite agenda of the churches and the educational institutions. Homes need the glory and the dignity they deserve by being once more restored back to centres of moral training. African society must be mobilised from within to appreciate the blessedness of the family of individuals of moral integrity. A nation is as healthy as its families.

Displacement due to wars and political unrest

Africa probably tops the world in the number of displaced peoples. Displacement may be due to one or the other of several factors: economic, political, social or cultural. Some displaced people become exiles or refugees in foreign countries, some move just beyond the borders of their countries. Others are displaced but remain within their homelands. Displaced peoples, for whatever reasons and whatever circumstances, are those people who have become uprooted from the only spots on earth they feel they have a right to call "home". They are expelled from familiar ground to which they have hitherto been attached.

The plight of African society due to political uncertainties and unrest is common knowledge. The refugee situation is very tragic. Uprootedness for whatever reason has adverse effects on the family. The stark reality is that family life is impracticable in the state of flight and the environment which a refugee camp is. Perhaps in this situation more than any other the family does become redundant when individuals have to run for their life. The crisis generated by war has become too perpetual in African society and many family members separated in the war never find each other. War atrocities mean that families are not only displaced but that they are hurting deeply. Survivors of cross-fires and genocide are not only grieving over the violent deaths of their dear ones ; they are also displaced, traumatised, lonely, bitter and vulnerable.

The very mass of traumatised humanity concentrated in refugee camps, and the total condition of war time where people die like insects, raise deep theological questions regarding the dignity of the human being and the sacredness of life. Even at the pragmatic level there is too much nakedness when in the camps women have to give birth in the open, when the polythene booths are see-through and when the only piece of undergarment has to be washed. In these circumstances women of whatever age have become extremely vulnerable to sexual assault and rape.

That the family institution is greatly devastated is not doubtful. When the end of political unrest, ethnic clashes and civil wars is not in sight it is difficult to talk about rehabilitating the family as an important institution of society. There seems to be a correlation between domestic violence and past experiences of displacement. [14]

This compounded problem necessarily calls for corporation of both the local and international communities. To the longing for peace must be added strong censorship of the arms industry and the politics involved at the local and international level. The grassroots community that longs for little more than normal secure family life is limited in its efforts without the involvement of influential sectors that can address the root causes of conflicts in Africa.

Poverty and family life

Poverty has many faces. Many problems that destabilise family life in Africa stem from poverty. That "poverty has no manageability" [15] can be appreciated because poverty drives its victims to lead lives which are contrary to their will.

Child labour, migrant labour for adult men and women, prostitution, and the problem of street children are some of the realities in African society that undermine family life.

Poverty has driven many young women into prostitution. It is a humiliating and dehumanising reality. Apart from the very high risk of contracting sexually transmitted diseases, including AIDS, a number of street children result from it. Street children are deprived of proper home life and as far as the future stability of society is concerned the reality of street children is a 'time bomb'.

Migrant child labourers are quite common in our society today. This is a time in Kenya where children are increasingly being employed as domestic servants, especially in urban areas. As such they have no experience of family life because they are answerable to their masters or mistresses. Often the media reports cases of child abuse in such situations in the form of beatings and other forms of assault. Growing girls, away from family protection have been known to be habitually sexually assaulted in the households where they labour. Such become adults who themselves bring forth children with no idea of what proper family life is.

In other instances child labour is employed in the agricultural sector, especially as pickers of tea and coffee alongside adult labourers. If the children sleep in their homes they nevertheless leave home early in the morning and return at dusk or after dark. As their counterparts in domestic service, they are subjected to a lot of stress.

The other category of migrant labour is of course adults themselves. Men especially started migrating into urban areas ever since the towns began to burgeon and grow under colonial rule. In Kenya colonial powers actually conscripted male labour to work on white settler farms during the first decade of this century with adverse effect on the agricultural communities who also required their menfolk for agricultural activities. The upheaval was bad enough to cause riots in parts of Kenya and to prompt some protests by missionaries. R.A. Barlow, for instance, protested about disrupted family life.

The demands of modern life and the dictates of economic realities have meant that a great number of menfolk are absent from their rural homes where their wives and children live. Whether they are in urban areas, in cash crop plantations or in mines and quarries, their long absences deprive families of male/father figures. The problems inherent in this situation are not difficult to find. First there is a crisis as the concepts of power and authority go through a process of adjustment and new meanings in the family context. A good number of men wake up rather belatedly to the realisation that they have alienated themselves from their children and that to their wives and children they may be able to exercise their power through command and masculine flexing of muscle but they have lost a good deal of authority and respect. Generalisations have their dangers but on the whole male absenteeism in contemporary African families has been known to precipitate a lot of conditions that work adversely for the welfare and well-being of the family. Some of these have to do with extramarital unions on both sides and mostly on the part of the men, with real fears of STDs including AIDS. Conjugal rights are simply not being taken for granted any more due to the anxieties inherent in the situation.

The other problem has to do with the shift of sympathies on the part of the growing children. Children grow up seeing only the struggles of their mothers who feed them, clothe them, prepare them for school, attend school meetings and so on. Father becomes a stranger who might find it very difficult to make a wedge for himself in the home he would like to call his. Sadly these are not hypothetical situations. Current studies in Kenya are revealing that family life is extremely jeopardised by situations such as here described and which kill or weaken the bond between family members.

When mothers are driven by necessity to become migrants the crisis is even more acute and complex. Sometimes they have to leave their children with relatives or to entrust the older children to look after their siblings. Either way in some cases this arrangement has led to deep resentments by the children and to cases of juvenile delinquency.

What hope for the family in Africa?

1. The participation of youth is critical for the rehabilitation of family life

This paper quoted elders at some length and indicated that the youth basically agreed with them that the breakdown of morality has adversely affected the family. Whatever the reasons for the instability of family life the youth and young adults are skeptical about the older generation's ability and genuineness to change things for the better. Young people need to be listened to and to be involved in programmes aimed at rehabilitating family life. In this respect, I quote a few representative voices from youth and young adults:

> The family is the basic unit of a nation. If things do not work in the family then the nation cannot be expected to function... Old people talk about young people being immoral, drug addicts, disrespectful, as aping foreign culture and not being proud of their own culture. They talk as if young people belong to another planet, as if they don't belong to the society. The older people forget they have played a role in moulding the society to be what it is. Young people are simply products of the society older people have created. The way they talk tells a lot about how mixed up and full of contradictions they are. [16]

Often students let off steam in the essays they write. One essay comparing traditional African education and modern education ended with a sentence that read, "I wish I was born and brought up in the African society that was!" One contribution to a global project for a better world by the Brahma Kumaris has this to say:

> It would be a pleasure to see a world full of love and harmony. I'd like to see the number of broken marriages reduce to zero and be sure that children are free from abuse. I would like to see the world as a community. (Alice Kingori, Student, Age 16, Kenya) [17]

This contemporary teenager speaks for many a youth in the African society. Family life is only meaningful and fulfilling where peace and harmony prevails so that marriages remain intact and children are secure.

2. Time is ripe for renewal

To reiterate the point already made, faith excludes despair and faith is built on testimony of things already seen. The family is an institution close to the heart of God. As a Christian I am persuaded that God's promises stand sure including the specific one to Abraham and Jacob regarding the families or nations of the earth (Gen. 12:3; 28:14). As an African I marvel at the resilience of the African peoples in the face of so much violence for several centuries. I see God affirming the family in the story of the Incarnation. As an African I appreciate the strong religious beliefs in the African peoples, the beautiful moral and societal values that still inform conduct especially in rural Africa. St. Paul captures the conflict arising from people's situations and many would say with him:

> For even though the desire to do good is in me, I am not able to do it... When I want to do what is good, what is evil is the only choice I have... Who will rescue me from this body that is taking me to death? Thanks be to God, who does this through our Lord Jesus Christ (Rom.7:18-25).

There are many unsung initiatives today at societal grassroots that are addressing this problem of contradictions. People long for good homes where they can fulfil expectations of kin and be themselves fulfilled. These initiatives need to be encouraged even as the unjust structures that set in motion these vicious circles are confronted.

Religions have a challenging and worthy task. Under God's guidance religions need to cooperate in tackling the evils that sap the life of the people, especially the family.

Hannah W. Kinoti

NOTES

[1] One of the common symbolisms is the umbilicus and it stresses that people are united in a fundamental way.

[2] To a number of African peoples such as the Ba-ila and the Gikuyu the woman's house and the granary are symbolic of the womb and fertility.

[3] The issues of domestic violence, including wife beating, killings, child abuse and rape by family members are well documented.

[4] A protracted court case in Kenya regarding where a prominent lawyer, S.M. Otieno, should be buried is relevant. The court ruled in favour of the rural home.

[5] N. Leys, *Kenya*, London, 1924, pp 189-190; W. Ross, *Kenya from Within*, London, 1927, p. 89.

[6] R.A. Barlow, quoted in H.W. Kinoti, "Aspects of Traditional Gikuyu Morality", Ph.D. Thesis, University of Nairobi, 1983, p. 88.

[7] *ibid.* p. 89.

[8] *ibid.*

[9] J. Kenyatta, *Facing Mount Kenya*, Secker and Warburg, London 1938, p.251.

[10] *ibid.*

[11] LAMB/1/6 University of Nairobi Archives.

[12] *ibid.*

[13] Kinoti, op.cit. pp.340-342.

[14] A current study in the Department of Community Health, University of Nairobi, is confirming this hypothesis but further analysis of results is required.

[15] This is a Gikuyu proverb meaning basically that because in poverty there are no resources to manage (exchange, distribute, utilize, etc.) the life of the poor drifts aimlessly without plan or control.

[16] Personal interview with Karimi Kinoti, Narobi, 22 June 1995.

[17] *Visions of a Better World*, ed. by the Brahma Kumaris World Spiritual University, 1994, p. 74.

The family in Judaism, past, present and future, fears and hopes

The central theme of Jewish religious life is that of sanctity. "For you shall be for me a kingdom of priests and a holy nation (Exodus 19 v. 6), God declares to the children of Israel as they are about to enter as a people into the Covenant at Sinai. You shall be holy, because I the Lord your God am holy" (Leviticus 19 v. 1), is the commandment that introduces the whole gamut of ethical and ritual observances of Jewish life. And the Midrashic work the Sifri explains the verses (Leviticus 22 v. 31-33) that read "and you shall keep my commandments and do them... and I shall be sanctified amidst the children of Israel, I am the Lord who sanctifies you, who brought you out of the land of Egypt to be your God..." to mean that God says 'for that reason I brought you out of Egypt, that you may he holy and sanctify my Name in the world'.

In other words, sanctification is the actual reason for the very existence of the Jewish People. It is thus not without significance that the Hebrew word for Jewish marriage (Kiddushiri) means "holiness or sanctification". Not only is the relationship of marital commitment itself seen as holy — indeed it is seen as the ideal state of adult life — but the family as the central institution and focus of Jewish life, is the key to the realization of the people's raison d'être, to be "a holy nation."

The central significance of family is seen by Jewish tradition as emphasized by the Bible in its narrative dealing with the trailblazer of ethical monotheism, the first patriarch, Abraham. Despite his pioneering achievements in bringing the knowledge of the one God, His Will and Ways, to the knowledge of so many others (as our sages interpret the phrase in Genesis 12 v. 5, "and the souls that they had made in Haran"), Abraham nevertheless yearned to be blessed with his own progeny; to have the full family network in which the profundity of spiritual and ethical commitment may be most fully transmitted. As stated in Genesis 18 v. 19, "For I have known him that he will command his children and his household after him that they will keep the way of the Lord to do righteousness and justice...".

It is this understanding of the spiritual meaning of progeny in the Bible, that illumines much of its narrative. The most particular example of this is the story of the binding of Isaac.

Not without portent then, it is the extension of the family of Abraham, Isaac and Jacob — known as the children of Israel — that becomes the nation. Indeed the nation is the sum total of its families and thus the nation lives up to its metier, when its families live up to their sacred task as sanctuaries of Jewish life. As the Rabbinic comment on the words of the gentile prophet Balaam puts it, "How goodly are your tents O Jacob, your dwelling places (literally - sanctuaries) O Israel" (Numbers 24 v. 5). Say the rabbis, "When are the tents of Jacob goodly, when they are 'the sanctuaries of Israel!'"

Indeed the central significance of family in the ethical purpose of the whole universe, is seen in the Genesis story itself. The initial creation of the human being singly — as opposed to all other creatures that are created in pairs at the outset — is itself understood in Jewish Tradition, to have moral purpose: namely, to teach that every human being is unique — a whole world in him/herself; and at the same time, that we are all descendants from the same one common ancestry (Mishnah, Sanhedrin, 4, 5). However the essential purpose of the narrative in describing the separation of the female part, to create two separate human persons, is expressed precisely in their reunion: "therefore shall a man leave his father and his mother and cleave to his wife and they shall be as one flesh" (Genesis 2 v. 24). The purpose of such is not just physical, but above all moral. Genesis 2 v. 18 reads, "it is not good that Adam should be alone, I will make a counterpart(ner) for him". The word "good" is used in the Hebrew Bible as a value judgment. In this context it is expanded by both the Midrash and the Talmud. In the Midrash, Pirke de Rebi Eliezer it states that the reason it is not good for man to be alone is "Lest it be thought that God is one alone in Heaven and man is one alone on earth". The Babylonian Talmud, (Ketubot 63) uses a more prosaic imagery in declaring that woman is a "counterpartner" for man in that, while "a man may bring home wheat, it is the woman who makes the flour and bread", and while "a man may bring home the flax, it is the woman who makes it into linen clothing". The fundamental idea behind these comments, as indeed the mediaeval Biblical commentator Seforno expounds on the Genesis narrative itself, is that mutual dependency is of essential moral value in preventing the dangers of arrogance — even self idolatry — and the delusion of self-sufficiency. Thus, even the natural physical relationship of a man and a woman is viewed as having the ethical purpose of instilling and nurturing moral values, which is the essence and purpose of the Jewish home itself.

It is the wife in particular who is seen as the central focus of the family and its religio-ethical purpose, to the extent that the Rabbis declare that the term "His house" (or better, "his home") means "his wife". And basing himself on the very language of the Biblical narrative, Rabbi Jacob in the Midrash Rabba on Genesis (17:2) says "He who has no wife, lives without good, help, blessing, or atonement"; and Rabbi Joshua of Sakhnin in the name of Rabbi Levi added "he is also without (real) life". Rabbi Hiya the son of Gamada says "he is not a complete man". And some say that he diminishes the Divine Image! These latter comments are of course based on the idea in the narrative, that it is only male and female together that make up "Adam", the complete human being, created in the Divine Image. Another Rabbinic comment extolling the moral virtue of marriage is that of Raba the son of Ulla who says that 'he who has no wife is without peace'. The sages say of he who loves his wife as himself and honors her more than himself and brings up his sons and daughters righteously and sees them married (in turn). "And you shall know that your tent is in peace" (Job 5 v. 24) (Babylonian Talmud, Yevamot 63a). (Here again, the focus of the "the tent", i.e. the home, is the wife.)

Naturally as the purpose of family is both to nurture the values of Tradition and above all to transmit the commitment for these to the next generation; the example that is set is of crucial importance. Our sages not only instruct us in detail regarding filial duty — in keeping with the fifth declaration of the Decalogue — but they themselves went to great lengths in this regard, serving as role models for future generations. For example the Babylonian Talmud (Kiddushin 31 b) tells of Rabbi Tarfon who would bend down so his Mother could use him as a footstool to get onto her bed. When he told his colleagues in the Study House of this with pride, they belittled his effort, telling him that when his Mother throws always all his money and he is able to hold his peace and not humiliate her in any way, then he can take pride in having fulfilled the commandment. That Talmudic text also refers to Rabbi Joseph who, when he heard his Mother's footsteps as she approached, would declare "I rise before the Divine Presence which is approaching".

Indeed the honor and reverence that the Bible requires children to show parents is seen within Jewish Tradition as bound up with that which we are required to express towards God Himself. The sages point out that the Torah uses the same injunction "you shall revere" for both parents and God; and similarly prohibits cursing both God and parents. This, they say, is because "all three are partners in creating the individual." Rabbi Shimon bar Yochai says "The Honor due Father and Mother, is so great (in importance) that God has made it (even) more important than His own honor. For it is written (in the Decalogue) 'Honor your Father and your Mother' without qualification, but it says (in Proverbs 3 v. 9), 'Honor God with your substance' (making the degree of honor) conditional on one's means" (Jerusalem Talmud Kiddushin, 1, 7). Furthermore the Fifth declaration of the Decalogue is the very connection between the commandments concerning our relationship with God and the commandments concerning relations between one person and another. Moreover, this is the command for which specific reward is promised — namely the prolongation of days on the land. Jewish tradition has expounded on the meaning of this, most importantly, in terms of the reward in the afterlife — the world to come. However, certain commentators have also noted the fact that the phrase promising longevity in the Torah is mostly in the plural, suggesting that it may refer to society at large. According to this understanding, the promise is emphasizing the crucial importance of a loving respectful relationship of children towards parents, for the ongoing survival and health of society as a whole.

As already stated, in as much as the family is the crucial cell of Jewish continuity and the fulcrum of its activity and purpose — overwhelming focus is placed upon the children as the vehicle of the continuity and this is already evident in the Torah (the Pentateuch) itself. Particularly notable in this regard is the command to bring the children to the public reading of the Torah by the King (Deuteronomy 31 v. 10-12) and especially the passage in the book of Deuteronomy, 6 v.4-9 that was identified by the sages, as the quintessential declaration of Jewish Faith and responsibility: which we recite in our prayers every morning and evening:

> *"Hear O Israel the Lord your God, the Lord is One. And you shall love the Lord Your God with all your heart with all your soul and with all your might. And these words which I command you this day shall be upon your heart. And you shall teach them diligently to your children…".*

The idea is further embellished powerfully in the Midrashic legend (Tanhijma, yayigash) that declares that when God was about to give the Torah to Israel, he asked for guarantors. The people of Israel offered the Patriarchs and then offered the prophets, but God did not accept any of them as adequate guarantors. But when they offered their children as guarantors, God accepted them as such and gave the people the Torah. In emphasizing that our values and way of life are guaranteed by our children — i.e., that our continuity depends above all on the future even more than the past — the Midrash also declares that our own faith and fidelity to it are measured by the extent to which we strive to ensure that our children are indeed "guarantors" of our posterity.

To this end the sages laid down directives accordingly. "As soon as a child is independent of his mother's care, he is old enough to fulfill the obligation of dwelling in a booth on the Festival of Tabernacles. If he knows how to wave the palm-branch, he does so. If he understands the commandments concerning fringes (on the four-cornered garment) and phylacteries and can put them on, it is his father's duty to provide him with them. As soon as he can speak, his father teaches him (to recite the text) "Hear O Israel", Torah and the holy language; otherwise it would have been better if he would never have been born" (Jerusalem Talmud, Hagigah, 1,2).

Rabbi Joshua ben Gamla receives particular accolade, in the Talmud (Bava Batra 21 a) for the procedures that he instituted to ensure the effective transmission of Jewish learning commitment and practice on a national scale almost two millennia ago. "Formerly" states the Talmud, a boy who had a father was taught Torah by him, while a boy who had no father did not learn. Later they appointed teachers in Jerusalem and boys who had fathers brought them along, while those who did not have fathers were still not brought along. Then they required that teachers should be appointed in every district, and they brought them lads of sixteen and seventeen. But when a teacher rebuked one of the lads, the lad would kick out and run away. Then Rabbi Joshua ben Gamla required that teachers be appointed in every district and in every town and that all boys be sent to them at the age of six or seven. Raba said: the number of boys for each teacher should be twenty five. If there are fifty boys they appoint two, if there are forty they appoint an assistant, "who is supported by the funds of the town..."

Of course, we might note in passing, that as ancient Israelite society was patriarchal, the major educational role was seen as applying to males, something which in subsequent times and especially in the last century or two has undergone great transformation, one might say, a revolution. Nevertheless, precisely because the major focus of Jewish life is the home and the family, it was always also considered obligatory to teach girls concerning all matters that pertained to home observance and devotion, celebration and commemoration. As a result, both Mother as well as Father, had a crucial educational role throughout the ages in Jewish life. Permit me to introduce a personal note on this point by way of illustration. While I grew up in England with English as my mother tongue, I could read and write Hebrew before I could read or write English, as — like millions of Jewish children before me — I was taught by my Mother to do so at the age of three, just as she taught me to say my prayers and to pay attention to matters of Jewish observance, from the moment that I started to communicate.

The purpose of this educational emphasis has already been noted. While respectful and loving relationships are both the foundation and purpose of family, the Jewish family has a holy purpose beyond itself and even beyond the social realm. Its purpose is to sanctify, through living God's Word and Way, all aspects of life. Accordingly as mentioned, the family is the central institution of Jewish life around which daily, weekly and annual religious observance resolves. For example, the Dietary Laws, the Sabbath, the Festivals, as major components of religious formation of the individual, focus overwhelmingly on the home and around the family table.

In the inextricable relationship between the family and the community, not only is the latter formed out of the former, but naturally the influences and trends within the community impact upon the family. For the majority of our history, extraneous influences were relatively minimal and generally did not pose any real challenge, neither to the identity of the community nor to the family. Indeed, the family was the focus of Jewish joy and light, warmth and compassion, in a society around us that was generally hostile and violent — a world that appeared to us down the centuries, as predominantly bleak and cruel. Paradoxically, precisely under such inhospitable circumstances there was no reason at all to fear for the future of the family.

The Enlightenment and emancipation of the Jew in the modern world, brought great and wonderful opportunities, facilitating the gradual integration of the Jew into an increasingly open society. However at the same time, it exposed him to arguably more insidious dangers. If it was not he whose way of life would be undermined by these, there was a good chance that he would lose his grandchildren to them. The very reverse of Balaam's curses which — though uttered as such — came out as blessings, according to Tradition; the blessings of modernity have sometimes proved to be curses.

Lest I overstate my case, let me make it clear that I am not seeking to romanticize the ghetto nor advocating an isolation from the wonderful and diverse richness — intellectual, cultural and scientific — that our modern world offers us. There are indeed some in our community who would do so; I would claim not only that this is undesirable as well as impractical, but even that to do so is to retreat from, if not to betray the fundamental ancient Jewish aspiration and obligation to contribute to the establishment of "the Kingdom of Heaven" on earth.

Nevertheless, I do not wish to minimize the attrition that threatens the Jewish family in the modern world. The more assimilated we are into society at large, the more difficult it is to maintain the way of life and values that are nurtured and transmitted through the family. Both the pace and demands of modern living, as well as the desire for cultural conformity, have led to an overwhelming weakening and ignorance of Jewish life, to the extent that the Jewish family is often a pale shadow of its former glory. This educational vacuum constitutes Jewry's major contemporary challenge!

As a result of such assimilation, the size of the Jewish people in the world today is constantly shrinking. Only in Israel is it actually growing. Of course, the latter is substantially affected by immigration, the return and relocation of communities in their ancestral land. However, even without these, the Jewish population in Israel is growing naturally, with a birth rate far higher than in the Jewish Diaspora where it is often below zero. Not least of all, Israel is the only place in the world where the dominant cultural ethos is Jewish, and thus where there is substantial protection from the aforementioned process of attrition.

Notwithstanding all these advantages however, in Israel too we face major educational challenges, where families are incapable or unwilling to assume their critical Jewish educational and formational role. This is both the result of tensions between Modernity and Tradition, as well as in the case of new immigrant groups like those from the former Soviet Union, the fact that they were victims over generations of a willful depravation of their heritage.

Furthermore, where Jews are acculturated to the most modern environment, then the changes in traditional roles and expectations naturally affect the Jewish family for better and worse. While women in particular are able today to enjoy increasing freedom of choice, not all men and women are able to adjust to this new reality; not all feel suited to it; and an increasing number seek alternative lifestyles. The Jewish community is thus confronted with escalating marital collapse and while Judaism never prohibited divorce, it was not a common occurrence amidst the strong and rich traditional family culture. Today in Western society, Jewish divorce rates are reaching the same levels as in the wider society. Moreover as indicated, the complexity of modern society also means that even aside from those who were the victims of marital break-down, there is an increasing number of single people in the Jewish community whose lifestyles are no long modeled according to the traditional Jewish family form and structure. Moreover the very mobility and con-comitant deracination within modern society, make traditional family life even more difficult to maintain.

One of the ways Jewish communities have responded to the challenge — especially in the United States — has been through the development of the community center, providing a broader base and framework for Jewish social and cultural involvement. Indeed there are many who argue that there should be less intense emphasis upon the family frame-work accordingly. Yet the view of traditionalists would be that while serious attention must be given to these new needs, no institution can ever fully compensate for the family as a spiritual center of Jewish life. While innovative frameworks need to be developed, these must not be at the expense of doing all we can to strengthen family life, as the most crucial cell that forms the national whole.

Naturally, the family is also challenged in contemporary society by modern technology, which knows no borders, and can intrude as never before, for better and worse, into the very heart of the home. As a result, an international imperialist culture of materialism and consumerism invades us today through TV, advertising and the proliferation of infor-mation, much of which does not deserve such a respectable title. This culture not only seduces people away from traditional observance and structures, but also generally preaches an ideology that is inimical to a religio-ethical world outlook that values, for example, moderation; not taking the world and what one has for granted; respecting another for what a person is and not how he or she looks or what they possess; com-passion for the needy and vulnerable; and not least of all, the human relationships and responsibilities that are especially nurtured in the family framework.

Yet it is precisely the traditional life of the Jewish family, which can provide the shelter and counterbalance for coping with this challenge — and surely the most notable expression in this regard is the Sabbath. It is the Zionist philosopher Ahad Ha'Am who is credited with the com-ment "more than Israel kept the Sabbath, the Sabbath kept Israel". Indeed, the Sabbath today is arguably more crucial than ever before for Jewish life — in particular, Jewish family life. In prohibiting technolog-ical innovation and activities on the Sabbath, Jewish Tradition has long ensured that even in ages of far more modest and limited technology (even when only relating to an agricultural society) the intrusions of human industry and economy would be barred from one day in the week. Accordingly, a whole day is set aside for focus not only upon family and community, but upon the rediscovery of inner-being, the human soul and its relationship with God and with His Creation as a whole. In the traditionally observant Jewish home, the intrusions of modern entertainment and consumerism are held at bay for one full day in the week, inculcating a sense of perspective, proportion and a scale of moral values. Moreover, in many a modern home, the opportunity for family to just come together in celebration, let alone to join in religious devotion, discussion and song, has become exceptionally rare. In the traditional Jewish family, this is a weekly event — a whole day of such devotion, strengthening the family bonds and nurturing a religio-ethical value system and world outlook.

Inevitably the Jewish world tomorrow will be a smaller one. Only those who substantiate their Jewish identity will retain it enough to pass it on to future generations. However, for that reason, while it will be smaller, it will also be stronger. We may draw some comfort in that knowledge and in the fact that Jewish life has always depended upon quality rather than quantity. Nevertheless, that does not release us at all from our sense of collective responsibility. There is indeed a widespread appreciation within the Jewish community of the educational challenge that we face today — and the extent to which we meet this challenge, is dependent upon the extent to which we empower the Jewish family as the principal educational framework, that ensures Jewish life, its purpose and destiny.

David Rosen

What apartheid has done to the African family and community and how the present situation can be transformed

APARTHEID can be traced back to the meeting of the indigenous people of our land and the white colonists. This was a meeting of people with entirely different worldviews and experiences. Their skin colours and life-styles were a result of generations of forebears living in two different climatic areas of the world. There was no superior or inferior group. Each was well equipped to deal with the harsh climates in which they found themselves. One clear difference of outlook was their concept of land ownership. To the African, with a broad extended family which included generations spurning time and eternity, land was regarded as communal property which belonged to ONE vast family — "few of whom were alive, many of whom were dead and countless of whom were yet unborn". How, then, could one family or individual claim exclusive ownership of land? A family could claim the right of use of land, but not exclusive ownership.

The colonists had a completely different concept of land ownership. To them land could belong to an individual or a family and could thus be retained or sold to another person or family in perpetuity.

The first discussions about acquisition of land were a monologue. Each party understood the other differently and each made their own conclusions. Conflicts about land ownership were confusing and, at the same time, destabilising to family and community and resulted in many wars between black and white, and between black and black.

The worldview of the traditional rural African is very close to the Jew's worldview. There are many striking similarities between these two worldviews, for example:

1. The role of the Ancestor, patriarch, or pater familias.

2. Polygamy.

3. The extended family.

4. Nomadic life — cattle and sheep farmers.

5. Sacrifices (birth, wedding, funeral, religious ceremonies)
   [Shrines used by both. The Jews later developed a synagogue and a temple.]

6. The Hand-washing ceremony.

7. Circumcision.

A society with this type of structure can survive many hardships and calamities. Racial rejection by others only helps the society to be more closely knit and not to change easily.

The period in South Africa, after mines were established, led to the growth of towns and rapid industrialisation. Urbanisation became a new feature for both black and white South Africans. Labour was needed and recruited in the villages, and even in the neighbouring countries, like Mozambique, Swaziland, Lesotho, Botswana and India. Before this period, labourers were slaves imported from Malaysia. During a recent visit to Malaysia I discovered that words which we regard as Afrikaans words actually came from the Malays — for example: Piesang, Piering, Pondoki.

The difference between white and black labourers was that whites were integrated into the new urban communities whereas the black were put in labour camps in the mines, or in hostels and dormitory camps called locations. The Africans were not like the Trek Boers. The men left the families in the village and commuted alone to the towns to work, and only returned to them after a long period. This type of lifestyle lent itself to exploitation. It also put severe strains on family life. Polygamous tradition encouraged the formation of several families or even resulted in immoral associations. This type of polygamous life was not typically African.

There was no Lobola and therefore no permanent unions between families. It was sexual life without responsibilities for the "wives" and children. It was a lifestyle without parenting, without care.

In this way, there was disintegration of family life in both the rural and urban societies. The responsibility of bringing up children fell to the mothers or to aged grandparents.

The inadequate wages had to be spread thinly among the scattered members of the families. The architects of racial separation, or apartheid, exploited this situation fully. They exploited the concept of HOME. To the African "home" did not mean the same as for the white westerner. Home was where the entire extended family lived. Some of the architects of apartheid were sons of missionaries or farmers who had lived near the African villages, and understood this world-view. It is not by accident that the policy of Bantustans, which sought to expatriate the Africans from the towns and cities to the rural villages came to be known as HOMELANDS. It was a vicious exploitation and distortion of the noble African concept of "home". The migration of Africans in large numbers during the long holidays like Good Friday and Christmas to their 'homes' gave credence to this philosophy. The Africans were unwittingly abetting their own oppression.

The origin and phenomenal growth of burial societies in the urban areas was due to this belief in "a home", away from town. For a long time the Africans did not accept burial of their people in the urban areas. Unfortunately it was expensive to transport people to their "homes" for burial. At first only children and poor people were buried in towns. Burial societies helped people to pool their resources to enable their members to be taken 'home' for a proper and decent burial. The ancestral village was HOME. Town was exile.

Psalm 137: By the river of Babylon there we sat and wept when we remembered Zion...

How can we sing a song of the Lord in a strange land?

On the positive side, the Burial Societies were also institutions of survival. There are very few institutions of a commercial nature that had the resilience of burial societies. They survived the rigours of the apartheid system and they made their members also survive the protracted apartheid siege. Today, burial societies are used for urban burials as well. The African funerals have become very expensive and difficult to organise because they are attended by many people. Burial societies enable families to organise their funerals with dignity and respectability.

It is worth mentioning, in passing, how the so-called 'funeral factor' brought about national survival as well. When political activity was paralysed by the vicious apartheid system, the only place where people could congregate was at a funeral (or wedding). When political victims increased, funerals became politicised. Funerals became larger and larger. The government became alarmed. Funerals, they decreed, must not be held on Saturdays but during the week, when many people are at work. The people voted with their feet. Instead of going to work, they attended the funerals. This amounted to work stoppages or strikes. The government changed this quickly and allowed Saturday funerals. The spirit of public resistance and mobilisation was fanned and maintained through the funerals.

The apartheid system was the most diabolical system of repression in the world. Elsewhere in the world it was maintained by individual prejudices, but in South Africa it had the full force of law to maintain it. The PASS LAWS were iniquitous and criminalised the people. This resulted in demographic engineering at a level unprecedented in the world. The PASS determined movement, employment, housing, education, and health services from the cradle to the grave.

The prisons increased in number and size, and were filled to overflowing. It was a curse to be black in colour. The whites had a superiority complex, which they believed had come from God. The blacks, on the other hand, began to develop an inferiority complex, which was damaging to their psyche. The blacks became foreigners in their own land. The word "native", which was commonly used at a certain time, developed a pejorative meaning. At a certain time, Africans from Mozambique, Malawi, and other states to the north of South Africa were called "foreign natives" — a contradiction in terms.

Apartheid was a system of absolute separation and therefore developed a geography of its own. People lived in different areas and blacks were located as far as possible from the town or city. To make matters worse even, the blacks were later sub-divided into ethnic communities. Blacks suddenly became different "nations" — the Pedi, Tswanas, Sothos, Zulus, Xhosas, Swazis, Vendas, Tsongas, Ndebele.

In contrast to these, the whites were one nation - English, Afrikaans, Germans, French, Portuguese, Spaniards, Italians, Americans, Swedish, Norwegians, Dutch, Swiss, Russians, later Japanese and Chinese. The Indians were a separate nation, and we even had the so-called Coloureds as a nation of their own.

Towards the end of the apartheid era, the country was becoming fragmented into different "governments" — about sixteen of them — with different parliaments, administration etc. This was divide and rule, or "divide and confuse" philosophy.

The worst thing about this racist philosophy was that it was given theological rationalisation and respectability. Many people were beginning to believe and swallow this perverted racial theology. Those who did not believe were gradually being conditioned to it. The churches in our country were sucked into this heretical theology, and ran their churches in this shocking manner. The last frontier of the racial war was fought in the church. It was when some churches and the church organisations declared apartheid a heresy that the apartheid ideology was turned on its head.

The New Dispensation has come with the inauguration of a new President and the new democratic, non-racial, non-sexist government. The moot question is whether this new government will eradicate apartheid in our country. To borrow a phrase that was used of Deism in the church — "Apartheid is dead but its corpse still stinks."

A system that was structured in a deliberate and thorough way cannot be changed by adopting a new constitution and passing a few laws. It will take the same thoroughness and intensity to change it. The biggest challenge to South Africa is how we have to change the hearts of the people. We have to teach the people how to accept one another and to live together in harmony. We have to change the superiority and inferiority complexes. We have to humanise our dehumanised people — both black and white. We have to revive Black-consciousness, White-consciousness and national consciousness. By this I mean the sense of being human and being proud of it. Not exclusiveness, but self and mutual affirmation. We need to revive UBUNTU. One writer describe Ubuntu in this way:

It is UBUNTU to love and care for others;
It is UBUNTU to act kindly to others;
It is UBUNTU to be hospitable;
It is UBUNTU to be just and fair;
It is UBUNTU to be compassionate;
It is UBUNTU to assist those in distress;
It is UBUNTU to be truthful and honest;
It is UBUNTU to have good morals.

A country that practises Ubuntu is the closest thing on earth to the Kingdom of God.

We need to encourage in our New South Africa healthy family lives and affirm the extended family and community consciousness.

Many religions operate well as a form of extended family — a caring community, a sharing community, a moral community.

We need to encourage all our religions to work together to transform our world, our global village, and heed the call of Cardinal Basil Hume:

"Throughout the whole of past history and forward into the future, the human family is called to be one in Christ and to manifest in creation the presence and the power of God's life and when the whole creation is caught up in a single symphony of love, the Kingdom of God will have reached fulfilment and God will be all in all. Until that ultimate realisation, the Church brings into unity those who in Christ have come to a new life of absolute love and a new vision of reality. Believers are committed to the building of a new city for mankind, a civilisation of love…"

Bishop Dr M. S. Mogoba

Tradition as a way to the future:
a Jewish perspective

The three components of our overall conference theme - family, community and tradition - form not merely a closely connected triad but actually constitute one theme in variations. In a sense, community and tradition may be regarded as horizontal and vertical extensions of family.

The anomie, the alienation, the rootlessness, the disintegration of the family, and the erosion of a sense of community, which we are witnessing in our depersonalized society, are not isolated phenomena but parts of a syndrome. They are all symptoms of the underlying malaise of our age: the excessive individualism which has so catastrophically impacted upon modern attitudes towards family, community and tradition. The ecological crisis which threatens the very survival of humanity has its roots in what I call the "ecological crisis" — the one-sided focus on the isolated and insulated individual. As Robert Bellah declared in his *Habits of the Heart*, "Modern individualism seems to be producing a way of life that is neither individually nor socially viable." (p. 144)

The epitome of secular modernity is best summed up in the formulations of the atheist philosopher Sartre, who declared "Hell is others" and "freedom is nothingness." This tragic finale is the logical conclusion of philosophies of life which reject all attempts to secure a transcendental foundation for human values. When ethical values merely represent purely arbitrary subjective commitments of individuals, any attempt to escape from the absurdity of the human condition is not merely an exercise in futility but an act of self-deception or bad faith.

The sense of meaninglessness is exacerbated under the conditions of our atomized mass societies in which individuals are reduced to mere ciphers. Lacking a sense of meaning and purpose, members of the "now generation" are condemned to a life of emptiness, revolving around the endless pursuit of instant gratification It is therefore hardly surprising that we are witnessing growing disenchantment with modernity.

This is one of the major reasons why liberalism has lost much of its popularity in the face of a rising tide of communitarian philosophies. The chaotic conditions of most urban centers, the high incidence of crime, the disintegration of the fabric of society have bred disillusionment and have intensified a nostalgic quest for the good old days. The formerly so widely held assumption that reason and science are capable of solving or at least ameliorating our problems has been found wanting. Contrary to the predictions both by Marxists and liberals that humanity will gravitate more and more towards the acceptance of universal values, we observe, even in the face of a global economy, the resurgence of particularism in the astounding impact of ethnicity and nationalism, especially after the cold war. What is especially relevant to this conference, the reversal of the fortunes of universalism and the revival of particularism have resulted in totally unexpected setbacks for the ecumenical movement.

While the yearning for the imagined tranquillity and serenity of more traditional societies is fully understandable, we must entertain an important *caveat* that, in the words of Thomas Wolfe, "we cannot go home again." We must somehow find a way between the Scylla of an extreme conservatism agitating for a return to an irretrievable past and the Charybdis of dismissing all traditions as an albatross around our necks. Such a third way should enable us to reconcile the revolutionary thrust of prophetic ideals with healthy respect for traditional structures and institutions.

This can be accomplished only if we recognize that the underlying cause of the disintegration of the very fabric of our society is modern individualism's failure to take seriously the insight of biblical anthropology, that "it is not good for man to be alone." With its focus on autonomy as the matrix of all values, it was taken for granted that, in the final analysis, individuals should be treated as self-enclosed entities. Biblical anthropology, on the other hand, stresses the human need for community. According to Genesis 2, woman was formed from man's side. Man is incomplete until he is re-united with the missing dimension of his existence. The primary goal of marriage is not reproduction, but the establishment of a true union with one's partner without whom one cannot be a complete person.

This conception of love and marriage sharply conflicts with modern notions. Whereas Freud wanted to reduce love to sexuality, eros to libido, the biblical view, as Paul Tillich has shown, relates love to the existential need for union with another self. Accordingly, the sexual impulse is no longer the foundation of love, but merely the instrumentality for bringing about the total union of husband and wife.

The ideal of biblical religions is *Deveikut* (attachment) rather than self-sufficiency or autonomy. Significantly, the first time this term appears in the Bible is in Genesis 2:24 with respect to the proper relationship to one's spouse. But the same term is also employed in Deuteronomy with reference to the ideal relationship with God that we ought to cultivate. The late Rabbi Soloveitchik brilliantly portrayed the human need for the establishment of a "covenantal community" with God in order to overcome existential loneliness.

The biblical conception of freedom also reflects concern for family and community rather than self-centered autonomy and independence. It may be symbolic that the Liberty Bell in Philadelphia contains only one part of the verse in Leviticus (25:19). "Thou shalt proclaim liberty to the land and all the inhabitants thereof." Completely ignored, however, is the sequel of the verse which spells out the real purpose of liberty. "It shall be a jubilee unto you; and ye shall return every man unto his family."

The sense of community advocated by Judaism is by no means limited to linkage with one's contemporaries, but extends to past and future as well. That is why on *Yom Kippur* we seek atonement not only for our own sins but also for those of our ancestors. The term *"Knesset Yisrael"* denotes a transcendent community. The Jewish liturgy pointedly refers to God not merely as our personal God but also as the "God of our fathers". Time and again Jews are admonished to remember, be it the Sabbath as a sign attesting to the divine Creation of the universe, the exodus from Egypt, the theophany at Sinai, the battle against the Amalekites, or various other specific historic events.

The emphasis upon the relevance of the past and the weight assigned to the authority of tradition is even more pronounced in the Torah's basic norm, "ask your father and he will declare unto thee, thine elders, and they will tell thee" (Deut. 32:7). In keeping with this orientation, the Talmud interprets the exhortation of the book of Proverbs (1:8), "Hear, my son, the instruction of thy father, and forsake not the teaching of thy mother," as implying the demand for reverence for established traditions of the community. In this spirit, Jewish religious law mandates adherence to *Minhag* (established customs and procedures).

This approach goes completely against the grain of the ethos of many Western societies which under the influence of utilitarianism or pragmatism worship progress and scoff at respect for traditional values. As Margaret Mead put it so tellingly, "the now generation has its roots in the future not the past." Or in the words of a well-known American poet, Robert Frost, "the past is a bucket of ashes." This is perhaps why an American witticism recommends, "Treat each day as if it were your first."

Whereas for modern man only the moment seems to be of significance, all biblical religions underscore the importance of the historic dimension. For all their fundamental differences, they focus on particular, contingent events such as Creation, Revelation and the establishment of Covenants. Small wonder, then, that early Christians recognized that their theological affirmations which were grounded in history were bound to constitute a "scandalon" to the Greek mind which could take seriously only what was validated by universally valid principles not by appeals to historically significant events. As Pascal pointed out, those who profess biblical religions worship, not the God of the philosophers, but the God of Abraham, Isaac and Jacob.

In contrast with the historic thrust of biblical religions, the Greek mentality preferred the realm of immutable laws of nature or reason over the merely contingent. Plato, for example, refused to bestow the honorific term "knowledge" on what was only grounded in sense experience. Even for Aristotle, there could be no knowledge of the particular or the individual, inasmuch as knowledge was made possible only by the assimilation of the "forms" of the entities encountered.

Hand in hand with this predilection for the universal and eternal goes the de-valuation of time in Greek thought. For Aristotle, neither the past nor the future were real. Time merely is the aggregate of now — the intervals between what is no longer and what is not yet.

As a religion based upon a variety of historic Covenants (from those established with the Patriarchs, to those entered into with the people collectively at Sinai and subsequently in the land of Moab prior to the entry into the land of Israel, and to the ultimate Davidic Covenant) Judaism was totally out of tune with the ethos of the Enlightenment, which tended to identify revealed religion with superstition and clamoured for the emancipation from what they regarded as the sole criterion of truth and value prompted the leading thinkers of the Enlightenment to reject any attempt to accord any weight to Revelation or tradition. This is why Kant went as far as to deny any religious significance to Judaism which in his opinion was nothing more than a mere legal code sanctioned by the tradition of a community.

So deeply ingrained was the aversion of the Enlightenment to religious traditions that the French Revolution, unlike most other revolutionary movements, never invoked the Exodus from Egypt as justification for its own struggle for liberation. No historic precedent could be of value to those who insisted that all institutions and structures must always be justified *de novo* by purely rational criteria — and not by an appeal to tradition or established practice.

That even nowadays it is widely assumed that a return to traditional values is not a live option is evidenced by Robert Bellah's assertion that even those who are completely disenchanted with modernity would view "a return to traditional forms... as a return to intolerable discrimination and oppression."

This identification of tradition with enslavement to the past represents the very antithesis of the tradition-directed approach advocated by religions that are based upon the belief in historic Revelations. Thus the Decalogue begins with "I am the Lord thy God, who brought thee out of the land of Egypt, out of the house of bondage." Many commentators took pains to point out that the historic experience of the Exodus rather than the belief in Divine Creation of the universe provides the foundation of the Jewish religion. For that matter, the observance of various holidays is primarily linked with the commemoration of historic events. In the Jewish liturgy reference to the Exodus from Egypt is made twice daily in fulfilment of the obligation to "acknowledge the yoke of the Kingdom of God."

The Exodus is also considered a precursor of the ultimate Messianic Redemption. Israel Ba'al Shem Tov, the founder of the Hassidic movement, went as far as to declare that "Remembrance is the beginning of Redemption." In a similar vein Rabbi Abraham Isaac Kook declared that the Exodus from Egypt will only be completed with the dawn of the Messianic era.

In his *Exodus and Revolution*, Michael Walzer adduces compelling evidence that, throughout history, the remembrance of the Exodus, far from fostering passive acceptance of the status quo, has actually inspired numerous progressive and revolutionary movements. It was precisely the memory of the past which captured the imagination of those who refused to reconcile themselves to the inevitability of oppression and injustice and prompted them to strive and struggle for a better future. The Exodus was viewed not as the culmination but as the beginning of a process leading to the attainment of perfect justice and dignity.

The Jewish tradition does not idealize the past, but regards its study as the source of guidance for the future. The events recorded in Genesis were treated as prototypes of future events. "What happened to the Patriarchs is a sign of what will happen in the future." Although the Torah is not a metaphysical or cosmological treatise, the account of Creation, according to the Midrash, was included because we can derive from it important normative lessons. Jewish thinkers stress that humans are given the task of finishing the work that God began with the creation of the universe.

It should be pointed out that the Jewish tradition does not look upon Revelation merely as a historic event that transpired in the past. Human beings bear an ongoing responsibility for the interpretation of the meaning of the divine Revelation for their time. There is a delightful Rabbinic story about Moses' inability to comprehend R. Akiva's hermeneutics of the text of the Torah. The very conception of the Oral Torah, for all its dependence upon MASSORAH (the authority of the tradition that is invoked to certify its authenticity) assigns a creative role to human beings in the elucidation of the meaning of Torah for their generation. It was this capacity for creative interpretation which enabled the Tannaim to declare a number of Biblical laws inoperative because they were intended for a totally different set of social conditions. Similarly, later authorities frequently stated that some of the provisions of Talmudic law were no longer binding on account of changed circumstances. This clearly shows that the belief in the immutability of a divinely revealed law by no means amounts to a tyranny of the past. The proper use of tradition involves not mere mechanical adoption, but the kind of appropriation which is sensitive to the requirements of modifications necessitated by the vicissitudes of the historic process. As T.S. Eliot put it, "Tradition cannot be had except by great labor." Recognizing the need for the dialectical tension between the heritage of the past and the demands of autonomy makes it possible to employ the insights of the past towards the building of a future, in which human beings will be adequate to the task of serving as partners with God in completing His Creation, Revelation and Redemption.

It is of the utmost importance for us to realize that a sense of historic continuity is indispensable to a meaningful life. As Samuel Pisar has expressed it, "we don't live in the past, but the past lives within us." To repress traditional values for the sake of an illusory emancipation from the bondage of the past represents an act of de-humanization. Without memory or anticipation, without a relationship to the time continuum that includes the past as well as the future, we lose our very humanity. We cannot exist merely as members of humanity in general. Our human- ity must be manifested in its very particularity. The Mishnah empha- sizes that, although each individual is endowed with the image of God, no two human beings are alike. Hence every person bears the image of God in a unique manner. The Bible does not mandate love of humanity as an abstraction. Instead, we are commanded "to love thy neighbor" in his/her particularity.

Modern history abounds with tragic examples of how the sacrifice of various national or ethnic traditions in the quest for universal religious, political or social visions has wrought havoc with numerous societies. As a Jew I deplore that in exchange for the Emancipation, it was expected that we surrender our distinctiveness. We were granted equal rights with the tacit understanding that we totally assimilate into the mainstream of European society. Similarly, many of the social problems plaguing the United States can be attributed to the "melting pot" phi- losophy which did not take into account the need of individuals as well as groups to maintain their respective traditions. Regrettably, many mis- sionaries, too, failed to take seriously the specific traditions of native populations, they expected converts to completely break with their past and swallow the entire Western culture, hook, line and sinker. This atti- tude gave rise to numerous totally unnecessary conflicts which devas- tated many native societies.

It goes without saying that committed as I am to transcendental, uni- versally valid values, I am not advocating a historicist position. But since the past lives in us, we must accept ourselves for what we are and real- ize that we form links in a historic tradition. It therefore behooves us to let our timeless ideals be filtered through the contingencies of our par- ticularity. It is only through linkage with our families, communities and traditions that we can embark on a journey that may lead to the acme of *Deveikut* (attachment) which can be reached by "those who are attached to God [and therefore] are fully alive" (Deut. 4:4).

Walter S. Wurzburger

Tradition as a way to the future: an African perspective

We begin with five African proverbs which will constitute the basis of our discussion. For, to us in Africa, proverbs are the daughters of experience and proverbs are also horses which carry us swiftly to the discovery of ideas:

1. One must come out of one's house to begin learning. And in this discourse, we are going to come out of our cultural and religious houses to begin a process of learning.
2. If you have not been outside of your home, you do not say that your mother's soup is the best.
3. Truth (knowledge or wisdom) is like a baobab tree, one person's arms cannot embrace it.
4. However big one eye may be, two are better.
5. Hunt in every forest, for there is wisdom and good hunting in all of them.

It is generally assumed that the traditions of African societies are veritable stumbling blocks in the way of what is called "development", and strenuous and relentless efforts have been made to transform the mentality and traditions of African people by those who want to pull Africa from what they understand to be Africa's "past", and bring it to the "present". Only the negative aspects of African traditions are often dwelt upon and the traditions themselves, in their entirety, are rarely seen as an asset. But it hardly needs stressing that the failure to adequately recognise indigenous cultures and their current or contemporary usefulness is one of the fundamental reasons for the failures and difficulties encountered in development work. The World Bank has come full circle to appreciate the value of what it calls "indigenous knowledge" and is making strenuous efforts at its collection, analysis and incorporation into its programmes.

Our traditions

By our traditions, I am referring to our cultural heritage which is peculiar to Africa - our way of life, our institutions, our religious heritage, mores, values, the way we came to terms with our environment and the many ways we devised to cope with it, the way we answered certain universal questions, such as the origin and destiny of humankind, the meaning and purpose of life, etc. It is these traditions which give us our identity and have been the basis of our creativity, inventiveness and innovation; they are not a thing of the past, on the contrary they have demonstrated a remarkable degree of adaptability and this gives them a necessary place in current discussions of development and the future.

The United Nations in its programme for the World Decade for Cultural Development, 1988-1997, has given recognition to the need to place culture at the centre of development. In its plan of action for the decade, the United Nations has four main objectives: acknowledgment of the cultural dimension in development; asserting and enhancing cultural identities; broadening participation in culture, and promoting international cultural cooperation. [1]

Development and the future

Broadly speaking, development means "the upward movement of the whole social system" [2] It means the systematic realisation of the full potentialities not only of the individual members within a society or nation, but also of the society or nation as a whole.

The early definitions of the concept of development were rather too materialistic and pure growth rates were used to assess the status of nations or societies to the exclusion of other factors. A developed nation was one which was characterized by economic productivity, high standards of living, technological advancement, political independence, the absence of basic human needs such as the need for food, shelter and clothing, etc. Societies or nations which were described as "underdeveloped" or "developing" were characterised by the absence of the characteristics which distinguished the developed nations or societies.

But I think development is not a monolithic entity and that there are many facets to it and attention must be paid to them if we are to appreciate and understand development in its full dimension. There are certainly aspects of development that are quantifiable, but these do not by any means exhaust the meaning of the concept. There are aspects of development that are non-quantifiable, but these should not be left out of consideration. Genuine development must be based on the concept of humanity in his or her full dimension and not on some aspect of his or her nature. Because development has to do with human beings, equal emphasis needs to be placed on material and non-material considerations, and ultimately, development should aim at a wholesome development of human beings and their societies. A developed society is one in which the material and spiritual aspects of humanity are made the basis of societal aspiration and are held in balance. It may be pointed out that from the perspective of the non-quantifiable aspects of development, such as in its human relations aspects, family ties, etc., some nations that are held out as models for others will be found to be woefully underdeveloped. This only goes to show that there is no such thing as absolute development.

The concept of development in our cultural heritage

It hardly needs stressing that the concept of development as an upward growth in all aspects of the social system is very much part of our cultural heritage. Natural objects such as trees, animals, etc., are each recognised to have a goal or fulfilment towards which they strive. Human beings grow from infancy into maturity and are socialized in the process.

Personhood is a process of becoming and each person is expected to grow or develop to his or her fullest potential, and traditional education which began when the child was in the womb, continued throughout the life of the person. Even after death, when the individual enters the land of the ancestors, who are believed to speak a bilingual language, education continues because the new arrival has to learn the language spoken in the land of the spirits.

At the level of the state, *oman*, in the Akan tradition of Ghana, the same ideas of desirable growth or development, *mpuntuo*, are present. *Mpuntuo* is a desirable end to which aspiration is directed, and the state is expected to move upward or forward in a desirable manner.

Another expression that is used for the same idea is, *oman no tu mpon*, the state advances or *oman no ko so:* the state prospers, grows, to attain certain desirable expectations, not only in the sense of the satisfaction of basic human needs, but also in the sense of the attainment of certain non-quantifiable goals, such as social peace, harmony, cooperation, mutual dependence, etc.

In the Akan tradition, every chief after enstoolment, swears an *ntam*, oath to his people in which he pledges to them that their welfare will be his concern at all times. And the chief can be removed from office for not honouring his pledge. He is removed because the Akan say, *mmre adwa, yenni nkaso*, no one sits for ever on the stool of time.

It may be added that during the imperial era of the Asante nation, the King's concern was not restricted to military conquest and territorial expansion. He had to see to what was called *amammuo*, refinement of government; *amansem*, the search for rational solutions to political issues as well as cultural development, *amammre*, among other things. All these responsibilities came under the rubric of *mpuntuo*.

Moving towards the future for me does not mean frantically trying to catch up with those whom we believe may be ahead of us; if there is any catching up to do in development for the future, it is with ourselves as a people by building on our own foundations. For, in every facet of human endeavour, aimed at the upward movement of the social system, there is a basis in our cultural heritage which can provide a foundation upon which to build; and we must endeavour to extricate ourselves from the venerable fiction that our inherited traditions, our culture, is opposed to scientific and technological development. If we are experiencing problems with moving our social system upward, the root cause does not lie in our traditions which are an inescapable foundation, it lies rather in the viciously crippling thinking which has been implanted in our heads and which we ourselves gleefully perpetuate, that we cannot advance ourselves or solve our problems without external assistance from the pace-setters, and that we can only build our nations on the basis of the intellectual concepts developed in Europe or America, and by doing so, we continue to lavish undeserved credit on Europe and America as if they had exhausted the limits of human possibility.

It hardly needs stressing that scientific creation is very much part and parcel of our cultural heritage and that the reason why this may not be too obvious to the casual observer is that, in our instance here in Africa, science became a cultural experience, firmly integrated into our way of life. In meeting the daily needs of food, shelter, clothing, health and education, knowledge of science was necessary.

Let me give a few examples to show the foundations upon which we can build.

Food preservation

After harvesting cassava, our people, in order to prevent it from rotting, resorted to many techniques. They turned the cassava into kokonte, by cutting it up into small pieces and drying them and later pounding them into powder which could last for a long time. Or, they could also grate it and fry it, turning it into gari. And, with regard to fish, they either smoked it, getting rid of the fat, or salted it, to preserve it.

Another way of preserving food overnight is to put a piece of charcoal in it to prevent it from going bad. If this is not done, and the food goes bad, the traditional folk explanation is that "a ghost has put its fingers into the food". This may be a folk explanation but underneath it is a scientific fact which is worth investigating. And that is, there is the ability of extremely small amounts of certain compounds to exert a lethal effect upon bacteria. A zone of inhibition is created around the charcoal, thus preventing the micro-organisms from growing and producing the undesirable flavour or odour compounds. Charcoal also has the ability to absorb odours. Thus when charcoal is added, it is able to absorb all the products of bacterial action which might contribute to undesirable flavour.

Hunting

In hunting elephants, our forebears knew that the huge creature has a strong sense of smell and that if a hunter got too close the elephant could trample him to death. And yet they had to hunt elephants with their bows and arrows, and doing so meant that the hunters had to overcome tremendous obstacles.

There are only two parts of the elephant's body that a hunter could hurt with a bow and arrow — the eyes and ears. If a hunter shot an arrow through the belly, the shot would be ineffective.

Our forebears therefore came upon two plants whose leaves when pounded together and smeared all over the hunters bodies, including their ears and nostrils, the elephant could not smell them. And having overcome the problem, all the hunters had to do was to ensure that the elephant did not see them. They could therefore stand a few feet away from the elephants and kill them.

Medicine

We have relied on medicinal plants, herbs and roots for centuries and even though Western medicine is available in many areas of Africa, we continue to use our herbal medicines because of their efficacy. Traditional medical practitioners still form the backbone of the health care delivery system in most African countries.

In our towns and villages in the rural areas of Ghana, people make fences around their houses and certain trees are usually found in the fences. A study of these trees shows that they all have immediate, medicinal value. For example, some of the commonest trees found in the fences are *abrototo* (Jathropa-curcas), *osensenema* (Neuboldia laevis) and *atoaa* (Spondia mombin). The juice from the Jathropa-curcas stops bleeding after a cut; the bark of the Neuboldia laevis chewed with rock salt, makes an effective de-wormer for children; while the bark of Spondia mombin is used for checking excessive bleeding after childbirth. Observation over the centuries has shown that when a pregnant goat or sheep starts chewing the bark of Spondia mombin, it is about to deliver.[3] The bark of the same tree is used as medicine to expel a delayed placenta, and for people who have delivered children in the homes for centuries, Spondia mombin becomes a first aid medicine right in the homes.

Some of our chewing sticks and chewing sponges have been found to check tooth decay, but one chewing stick in particular, fagara xanthoxyloides, locally known as *Oshogbo* chewing stick in Nigeria, has been found to have properties that appear to combat the distortion of blood cells typical of sickle cell anaemia, a hereditary disease affecting primarily people of African descent the world over. Preliminary trials of the sickle cell neutralizer were conducted among patients at the University Teaching Hospital at Ife. The pharmacologist, Dr. Sofowora, said: "Patients have been reporting to us since they have started taking this extract for some 15-24 months. They have not had to visit the hospital because of crisis. Normally, these are patients that twice a week have to rush to the hospital when they go into sickle cell crisis".[4] A medicinal plant research team at Nsukka in Nigeria has also developed cajuminose. from a local tree, cajanus cajan, for the treatment of sickle cell anaemia.[5]

Mention must also be made of the Madagascar periwinkle, the pink and white periwinkle, which many of our herbalists in the rain forest areas use as a remedy against diabetes. Following this lead, biochemical researchers in the West studied the plant and found that its alkaloids contain an unsuspected weapon against cancers and out of this, two anti-cancer drugs have come out.[6]

One of the most recent examples of the lead our herbalists can provide for the development of medicinal research in Africa is the work of a consultant surgeon and lecturer, Dr. Spencer Efem, at the University Teaching Hospital in Calabar, Nigeria. Dr. Efem has, since 1984, successfully used honey, straight from the bee-hive, to treat wounds, including burns, deep bedsores and various types of ulcers. According to a report in the 7 July 1988 issue of the *New Scientist*, "This is the first time that it has been demonstrated that honey can be used to remove dead tissues from persistent wounds instead of stripping them away surgically."

Dr. Efem himself explains the curative powers of honey:

Honey is acidic and destroys bacteria. It is extremely hygroscopic, which means that it is a dehydrating agent, and can therefore destroy bacteria just by removing fluid from them. It also contains an antibacterial agent called inhibine. It also contains vitamins and minerals which improve the nutritional status of the patient.[7]

This is a fantastic breakthrough, but Dr. Efem is not stopping here. He is carrying out sensitive laboratory tests on all known organisms that cause wound infections to determine which of them can be destroyed by honey. He is also carrying out similar research on fungi, the major cause of many infections in the tropics.

In his book, *African Ethnomedicine*, Dr. Maurice Iwu of the University of Nigeria, Nsukka, makes the salient point: "What we want our government to understand is not to compete with the West in chemical synthesis but to analyse our own flora and fauna".[8]

Dr. Iwu and a team of medicinal researchers have made a notable breakthrough in their study of bitter kola or *Garcinea kola*, for the treatment of liver diseases. Bitter kola is daily used by people in that part of the world as elsewhere in West Africa. Extracts from bitter kola as well as seeds gave remarkable improvement of liver function in patients with chronic hepatitis and cholangitis after treatment for fifteen days at a Nigerian herbal home. The team has subsequently manufactured *Hepavos* capsules from bitter kola for the treatment of liver diseases.

At the Centre for Scientific Research into Plant Medicine, at Mampong in the Eastern Region of Ghana, Dr. Oku Ampofo and his researchers, taking their cue from local herbalists, have been treating diseases from local plants:

(a) *Cryptolepsis sanguinolenta* — has been used in the treatment of fevers, urinary infections and upper respiratory tract infections.

(b) *C. Sanguinolenta* — has been used in treating malaria fever.

(c) *Desmodium Adscendens* — for the treatment of bronchial asthma, dysentery, wound dressing and colic.

(d) *Clausena Anisata* — for toothaches, rheumatism, headache, migraine and snake bite.

It is also used for the treatment of impotence, sterility and as a laxative after child birth.

(e) Bridelia Ferrugumea - for fever, headaches, rheumatic pains and as a mouthwash.

(f) Indigofera Arrecta — the leaf extract is used at the Centre at Mampong for the treatment of maturity onset diabetes meillitus. A report further added:

In preliminary clinical evaluation of patients receiving the leaf extract of *Indigofera Arrecta* in three daily doses after meals, it was found that the majority of the patients improved clinically and their fasting glucose levels dropped from an average of 250 to 120 mg. and the post-prandial glucose levels were corrected. It was also noted that the oral glucose tolerance curve changed from the typical diabetic to the normal in about three months. From our preliminary data, the leaf extract of *Indigofera Arrecta* seems to possess interesting anti-diabetic properties and thorough investigation. [9]

All these breakthroughs would not have been possible if the researchers had not followed the lead of our traditional medical practitioners. And traditional medicine provides a foundation upon which we can build for the future and our medical students trained locally would be better doctors if they were exposed, in the course of their training, to our traditional medicine in addition to Western medicine. They will thus stand on two legs instead of one. But who says standing on one leg (Western medicine), is better than standing on two (African medicine and Western medicine)?

The most unscientific statement is the oft-repeated assertion that "African medicine is unscientific". For how does a scientist condemn or reject something without investigation? Or, is the traditional medical system branded unscientific merely because it cannot be integrated within present-day scientific concepts and terminology? It is a fact that our medical specialists have been trained to know more and more about less and less and do not therefore have the necessary training and intellectual capacity to cope with traditional medicine. [10]

Of course, traditional medicine is not foolproof, no medical system is foolproof, anyway. But if we have a dual medical heritage, wisdom dictates that we use both. My plea for traditional medicine is not based on the fact that it is cheap and easily available or that it will save us scarce foreign exchange resources. My point is that it has been proved to be effective and more research will reveal more startling results.

A look into our traditional culture to find scientific bases alone does not exhaust our task. Indeed, we need to recognise that the relevance of our traditional culture for contemporary development and the future will be discovered when we continuously engage in the sustained effort to find what from our traditions can be used to provide a basis for inspiration and construction of the present and the future.

Preservation of the environment

An important aspect of our cultural heritage is the preservation of the environment, and there are innumerable taboos and restrictions whose meaning may elude us precisely because we have not taken the trouble to go into them to discover their usefulness or relevance for our contemporary as well as our future life. Our forebears recognised that life would be robbed of part of its essential meaning if people did not respect or even revere the environment around them.

Characteristic of our traditional culture is reverence for nature and our oneness with it. To enforce this reverence, there are many prohibitions, all aimed at preserving nature, for "Nature is not just an object, but a tangible reality from which humanity derives its sense of wholeness and well-being".[11] Fishermen do not go fishing on Tuesdays in Ghana and this gives the ocean a day of rest to replenish itself; the fishermen also get a day of rest to mend their nets. People are forbidden to till the earth on certain days of the week, and this is to show respect for Mother Earth.

Fishermen are expected to "sacrifice" some of their catch to *Bosompo*, the god of the sea, after each fishing expedition before returning home. The fish that are sacrificed must be live fish, not dead ones and an Akan maxim which supports this ritual says, *"Bosompo ankame wo nam a, wo nso wonkame no abia "* — if the god of the sea does not begrudge you of his fish, you do not begrudge him of your catch. The fish the fishermen sacrifice to the god of the sea will continue to breed and there will continue to be fish in the ocean, if this ritual is observed. It is therefore taboo for a fisherman not to make a sacrifice, and the concern for the environment expressed in the ritual sacrifice is quite evident.

In the farming areas too, it is taboo for anyone to bring home a whole bunch of palm fruits from the farm. One is expected by custom to cut a bit of the palm fruits and leave them on the farm before returning home. This is an expression of gratitude to Mother Earth for the harvest made. But underneath the taboo is the idea that every palm fruit which is brought home is going to be boiled or cooked and the kernels will not germinate. But the palm fruits left on the farm or forest will germinate and grow into palm trees and provide food, not only for the present generation, but also for future generations. Those who did not observe this taboo were regarded as a threat to human society and were dealt with accordingly in the past.

The importance of this taboo is not diminished by the argument that squirrels and crows which feed on ripe palm fruits propagate the seeds and therefore render the taboo of no consequence in "modern" times. This argument ignores the fact of human responsibility towards the environment which is inherent in the taboo. It is not the responsibility of crows and squirrels, or for that matter, any other animal, to ensure human survival and ecological balance. It is human responsibility and that is why infringement of the taboo was taken seriously in the past.

We may ignore the taboos and restrictions, but we dare not miss the salutary lesson our forebears wanted to teach us through them. True and meaningful growth must go hand in hand with respect for the environment, a fact which the modern world has finally come to recognise. Our traditional attitude to the environment is not only valid but actually essential for the future of the world.

Values

In any meaningful discussion of the future, we cannot ignore our African sense of values, for it is within the context of values that choices and decisions affecting the future are made. As a result of Africa's contact with the external world, other values have come to be planted on African soil and there are Africans who assume that the goals for our future have already been defined for us by the colonial powers which colonised our countries and also by the agents of the guest religions — Christianity and Islam — who have planted other values.

We cannot, of course, live in isolation from the rest of the world. We may borrow ideas we need from other places but hold on to the undercurrent of our African traditions and integrate them into our own and make them serve African survival and prosperity.

Our traditions place a high premium on personal relations and to be human is to be in relation with others. The extended family structure is the outcome of this value and is an answer to loneliness. The extended family which has been severely criticised need not be an obstacle in our journey to the future. On the contrary, it has enormous potential in enhancing human development and the cultivation of humanistic values, feeling for one's fellow humans, without which no society can survive and function efficiently. It may be pointed out here that the cocoa industry in Ghana, which attained international fame, derived its strength and impetus from the traditional organisation of the Ghanaian family.

Within the framework of the family is the special place for old people, who are cared for as a matter of obligation. Traditionally, the old are the educators of the young and since a person's worth is not determined solely in terms of his or her economic productivity, the elderly do not lose the respect and reverence due them. People therefore look forward to old age, not with fear and trembling, but with confidence, that they will be useful to society.

There is a moral reason for this attitude and it is that since everyone hopes to be old some day, one should not molest any old person now for the sake of vengeance; hence the maxim, "He who aspires to be old should not take the old man's walking stick from him". The walking stick is the old man's support and personal adjustment. Another proverb which reflects this feeling of obligation is, "If your parents take care of you up to the time you cut your teeth, you take care of them when they lose theirs".

The value of the elderly as a source of reference and guidance is expressed in the proverb, "The one who does not have an elderly person in his or her home must be pitied"; while the proverb, "Everybody has been a child before but not everyone has been an old man or woman", emphasizes the value of experience.

In our traditions, wealth is determined not so much by the number of things a person has, but rather by how many people a person has around him or her. The happiness of a person is directly linked to the amount of attention and love which come to him or her from other people. And in this regard, the elderly are the most blessed, for they are in the most visible position to receive a lot of attention. Children, too, receive a lot of attention because they belong to the whole community.

Human beings are prized above all else and the following may be cited to illustrate this particular point:

> "It is man that counts; I call upon gold, it does not answer, I call upon drapery, it does not answer, I call upon man and man answers. It is man that counts!"

> "Lack of people (companionship) is worse than lack of money".

> "A house with a bad person in it is better than an empty house".

> "A human being is more beautiful than gold".

But the human being who is prized, is also a member of a community and it is in community that a person realises himself or herself. To be human is to be in relation with others — dead, living and those yet to be born. Living in community implies that cooperation rather than competition is emphasised as a social value.

Confidence in the ultimate victory of truth over error and falsehood which is the cornerstone of traditional moral education, is expressed in the following proverbs:

> "Whereas a liar takes one thousand years to go on a journey, the one who speaks the truth follows and overtakes the liar in a day".

> "Truth swallows (is not afraid of) bullets".

> "If you dig a hole deep into the bowels of the earth and bury truth there, it will come out by itself (you will not have to dig for it)!

There are moral foundations in our traditional culture which are relevant for our contemporary life as well as our future well-being in Africa. Indeed these moral foundations are the only sound basis on which to build our future; and although we live in an interdependent world and must borrow from others, what we borrow must come to embellish what we already have and not to supplant it.

Conclusion

Finally and incomparably, I want to suggest that we cannot have a future as a people without self-acceptance, self-awareness and self-confidence, all of which take their source from our cultural heritage. This is the foundation bequeathed to us by our forebears and it is from this foundation that we can derive the strength to feel maximally secure in our thoughts and remain unassailably ourselves and assume, henceforth, the entire responsibility for our destiny.

We have to accept ourselves without apology in direct and forceful opposition to the seemingly inflexible thinking which aims at putting us at a disadvantage, merely for who we are, on the basis of some spurious logic; and say with Archbishop E. Milingo of Zambia:

"If God made a mistake in creating me an African, it is not yet evident".

Our task is to change our minds about ourselves in order to lay hands on the greatness which is our own inheritance. Our journey to the future began in Africa and its destination is in Africa, not in Europe or America. Our ultimate destination will be slightly different if we maintain our originality and integrity. I am convinced that we do have assets, only we have not educated ourselves into an awareness of them on our journey towards the future.

I will let our ancestors have the last word, although we say in our proverb: "Onipa didi wie, na onwie kasa", literally, we finish eating, but never finish talking. When our ancestors wanted to encourage us to make use of what we have or take the blame ourselves if someone takes it away or destroys it, they got their idea from the harmattan and what we have to do to prevent our lips from drying up and becoming chapped or cracked: "The man who does not lick his lips, cannot blame the harmattan for drying them".

Kofi Asare Opoku

NOTES

[1] *A Practical Guide to the World Decade for Culture Development, 1988-1997*, Paris: UNESCO, 1988, p. 16

[2] Myrda, Gunnar, *Asian Drama: An Inquiry into the Poverty of Nations*, New York: Pantheon (3 vols).

[3] See, Kofi Asare Opoku, *Primary Health Care Within the Context of our Traditions*. Pamphlet Box, Institute of African Studies, University of Ghana, Legon, Ghana.

[4] *The Mirror*, Ghaija, November 13, 1982, p. 3.

[5] *West Africa*, No. 3698, June 27 1988, p. 1156.

[6] *Reader's Digest*, July 1982, p. 125.

[7] *West Africa*, No. 3715, October 24-30, 1988, p. 1994.

[8] M. Iwu *African Ethnomedicine*, as quoted in *West Africa*, No. 3698 June 27, 1988, p. 1156.

[9] Oku Ampofo and Boye, "The Role of Traditional Medicine in Primary Health Care in Ghana", in *The Use of Herbal Medicines in Primary Health Care* (Proceedings of a meeting organised by the Christian Medical Commission, September 1-5, 1987. Lomé, Togo), edited by R. Amonoo-Lartson.

[10] M. Iwu, *African Ethnomedicine,* as quoted in *West Africa*, No. 3698, June, 27 1988, p. 1156.

[11] *Religious Experience in Humanity's Relation to Nature: A Consultation* (Yaoundé, Cameroun/Geneva, 1978), p. 14.

Yaound 2001

Travel report

African Christian-Jewish consultation in French-speaking Africa - Hans Ucko, 8-13 November 2001, Yaound ́ , Cameroon

Jewish-Christian dialogue is in Europe and North America a well-established experience. It continues to inspire many Christians, which is demonstrated in many church documents and theological writings. Lately it has also led to a reflection on the role and significance of Christianity for Jewish theology. I have referred to the document Dabru Emet in an earlier travel report. The Jewish-Christian dialogue builds upon the presence of Jewish communities and the problematic history between Jews and Christians in Europe. Anti-Judaism and antisemitism have left stains in history impossible to remove and impossible to forget.

There is of course another aspect of Jewish-Christian encounters or rather lack of encounters. The Israeli-Palestinian conflict is one major reason for the absence of dialogue between Jews and Middle East Christians. The Middle East Council of Churches (MECC) responds coolly to suggestions from Jewish or Jewish-Christian organisations to engage in any Jewish-Christian dialogue, lest it be interpreted to support the cause of Israel.

Christians in other parts of the world, where there is no or insignificant Jewish presence or history, are not immediately part of the Jewish-Christian dialogue. They may for sure have other priorities. If there are any associations with Jews and Judaism, they are complex and contradictory. They may be related to what is said in the Bible about the Jews. They may refer to what was conveyed through missionary education. Attitudes encompass respect and esteem for the chosen people, the people of God but entail alas also classical theological positions between Jews and Christians expressed through polarisations such as old and new, Law and Gospel, merit and grace. There is the sympathy for Palestinians, living under occupation by the Jewish State. At the same time there is also in some places, where Islam is dominant and Christians live as minorities, a silent support for Israel in its struggle against Muslim neighbours, Israel vicariously doing what they would like to do themselves but cannot do.

The desk for Jewish-Christian relations has the mandate to bring into the Jewish-Christian dialogue Christian partners, for whom there are no immediate encounters with Judaism or Jewish communities. There have thus been Jewish-Christian dialogues organised by the WCC in Nairobi 1986, in Hong Kong 1992, in Cochin 1993, and in Johannesburg 1995.

Some of them have been co-sponsored by the International Jewish Committee for Interreligious Consultations (IJCIC), an umbrella organisation of mainly American Jewish bodies.

The consultation in Yaoundé was the result of a collaborative effort between IJCIC and WCC and is the first Christian-Jewish dialogue organised in French-speaking Africa. Aside from this fact, it is worth noting how many of the African Christian participants welcomed that the WCC, as they said, finally took note of French-speaking Africa.

The consultation was carefully planned with the IJCIC consultant in Geneva, Prof. Jean Halpérin, and in an ongoing communication with the WCC and All Africa Conference of Churches staff, facilitating the choice of themes and suggesting participants from WCC member churches.

The consultation was divided into three themes: Shalom and ubuntu; Memories and experiences of violence; The challenges to peace-builders.

The Protestant Theological Faculty in Yaoundé provided the venue and assisted in logistics. There was a particular interest at the Faculty for things Jewish. A former Israeli ambassador to Cameroon had for many years set aside time to lecture at the faculty and give talks in parishes. The words in Hebrew on the entryway to the faculty compound, Emunah (faith and trust), Dat (knowledge) and Edut (witness) were thus a sign of an interest in Hebrew, the Old Testament and Judaism and expressed the interaction that was to become the significant feature of this dialogue.

African participants represented both church and university in Benin, Burundi, Cameroon, Congo Brazzaville, Côte d'Ivoire, Democratic Republic of Congo, Kenya, Rwanda, South Africa and Togo. The Harrist Church and the Kimbanguist church represented the African Instituted churches (AIC). The representative of the Harrist Church expressed at several occasions that there was a particular affinity between Africans and Jews. Many of the AIC churches understand themselves to be photocopies of the People of Israel and identify themselves with the Jewish people in their own calling to be a people set aside with a particular mission. Other African participants echoed the same. Europe had exported its history of antisemitism to Africa, but it had no place in Africa. Moses was an African, he married an African. He spent a major part of his life in Africa. He was before the exodus according to tradition the sovereign of Ethiopia. The Jews were for many years slaves in Egypt, thus in Africa. There is an alliance between Africa and the Jewish people. One of the African participants told the story about his own people, who walked forty kilometres to meet him after they had learned that he had been to Jerusalem. One of their own coming home from Jerusalem was something out of the ordinary. The Old Testament, the Holy Land, and the People of God are loaded concepts in the African Christian tradition. During worship in church at the time of our consultation, there was immense jubilation as people learned that one of the

Jewish participants actually came from Jerusalem. There was no end to the praise and ovation.

Jewish participants came from France, Israel, Switzerland and the United States. A Jewish and a Christian participant represented the International Council of Christians and Jews (ICCJ). There were in all 25 participants.

Every morning was ushered in through a common Bible study. The first Christian Bible study on the Pharisee and the Publican (Luke 18, 10-14) could easily have collapsed the consultation from the beginning. The Bible study used all the stereotypes that those involved in the Jewish-Christian dialogue have learned not to use and why not to use them. But the Jewish participants understood that the stereotypes were not there to hurt or offend. They were simply part of a traditional Christian "teaching of contempt" carried along without much conscious reflection throughout the oikoumene. This traditional teaching sees the Jew more as a theoretical theological construct illustrating a polarised Christian teaching than a person of flesh and blood, a person in his or her own self.

Instead of leading to a polarisation between Jews and Christians an interesting discussion took place on the concept of fasting, where the text from Isaiah (58, 3ff) became significant, a text also used in the Yom Kippur service.

Why do we fast, but you do not see? Why humble ourselves, but you do not notice? Look, you serve your own interest on your fast day, and oppress all your workers. Look, you fast only to quarrel and to fight and to strike with a wicked fist. Such fasting, as you do today will not make your voice heard on high. Is such the fast that I choose, a day to humble oneself? Is it to bow down the head like a bulrush, and to lie in sackcloth and ashes? Will you call this a fast, a day acceptable to the Lord? Is not this the fast that I choose: to loose the bonds of injustice, to undo the thongs of the yoke, to let the oppressed go free, and to break every yoke? Is it not to share your bread with the hungry, and bring the homeless poor into your house; when you see the naked, to cover them, and not to hide yourself from your own kin?

A particular feature of this consultation was living together the worship life and holy day of the other. Christians participated in the Sabbath service and were guests of honour at the Sabbath meal and the Jewish participants took part in Sunday worship and the ensuing get-together. This proved to be very much appreciated by both Jews and Christians. The Christian participants were instructed in the flow of the Sabbath service and guided throughout. The Sabbath meal was prepared by staff from the Israeli Embassy and provided the traditional East European Jewish standard dish gefilte fish (close to the equator!), wine and Sabbath songs. Sunday morning found Christian and Jewish participants in a very lively Christian worship with singing and dancing. It is worth noting the reactions of some the Jewish participants: "The heritage of suspicion is not present here. I have never been so at ease in a church as today." "I entered the church with some reservation, but never before has participating in a Christian worship been so meaningful." "It was a luminous idea to have Jews and Christians sharing their respective celebrations." Such live-in features had a remarkable impact on the dialogue and are something worth taking note of beyond the consultation in Cameroon.

This is not the place to summarise the content of the presentations and the ensuing discussion on the themes. The evaluation of the consultation resulted in a commitment to work towards a publication of the material together with studies of biblical sources, which refer to the African people, and seeks to create a Jewish-African anthology. Reference was made to a publisher in Paris, specialising in Africa. I will instead highlight only a couple of issues that were important in the consultation. Although not directly an activity of the Decade to Overcome Violence, it became obvious how much we could refer to the Decade as an incentive towards peace making, towards shalom and ubuntu. To pursue peace is more than to love peace, anyone can love peace, but to pursue peace is to create peace. Shalom has to do with the verb shalem, which means to pay. There is effort involved, one has to pay one's dues, and one has to be released and acquitted from one's debts.

Ubuntu is that which makes our humanity, all that which makes the human being different from the animals. A person, an individual should be ubuntu, playing his/her given role in the community, assuming responsibilities. "It is ubuntu to love and care for others. It is ubuntu to act kindly to others. It is ubuntu to be hospitable. It is ubuntu to be just and fair. It is ubuntu to be compassionate. It is ubuntu to assist those in distress. It is ubuntu to be truthful and honest. It is ubuntu to have good morals. A country, which practises ubuntu, is the closest thing on earth to the kingdom of God." It is through the word, the palaver (the reunion of the clan to talk about a crisis in community, re-establishing broken relations) that there is a possibility to pursue peace. In this participants saw likeness and relationship between shalom and ubuntu through the importance of the word against violence. The palaver is the tool in a conflict. The palaver distinguishes the human being from the animal. The absence of the word opens for violence. The Truth and Reconciliation Commission had as a principle to give both camps the word, the possibility to speak. Reconciliation must precede peace.

A peak in the consultation was in the discussion about memories and experiences of violence. Here Shoah and Rwanda became the focal points.

The churches involved in violence live between being victims and being responsible, between memory and amnesia. In this situation, one cannot operate with a theology of liberation. A theology of reconstruction is needed. Everything was shattered after what happened in Rwanda. African cultures and values were shattered. The words of

Ezekiel 37:11 echoed in the wake of Rwanda, "Then he said to me, 'Mortal, these bones are the whole house of Israel'. They say, 'Our bones are dried up, and our hope is lost; we are cut off completely.' "

The discussion on the topic took off in how we are to deal with our memories, whether one can allow oneself to forget in order to live, whether this would be the same as forgetting the crime which was committed. Is forgetting an act of humiliation of those who died and those who survived and who want to know who killed their parent, child, relative, or friend? The words of 2 Samuel 21 (David avenging the Gibeonites) played into the discussion. How does one safeguard the memory and at the same time keep a way out for pardon and forgiveness?

African theology has dealt with both memory and violence. Memory is foundational and is celebrated in a liturgical manner in the theology of reconstruction. Countries, cultures, dignity have been destroyed repeatedly and yet one has to assume the responsibility to deal with memory in a constructive way.

There is a need to think in terms of reparation and not in terms of retribution. Or else, the whole population is imprisoned. One needs to find a way of symbolic punishment in order to live together. A sort of Truth & Reconciliation Commission is needed, but how does one prepare people for it?

There is of course a need for a conventional code of "human rights" that would serve as a legal instrument for detecting, measuring, and redressing injustices. Yet, the greatest weakness of a theory of justice revolving solely around human rights is that it creates an ethos in which there is no room whatsoever for forgiveness and reconciliation. The correct but incomplete theory of justice has made us unable to forgive or forget the endless list of grievances we attribute to the other party. As long as we only fight for our rights, we shall continue to fight against the other. In the vocabulary of the "human rights language", the words "repentance, forgiveness and reconciliation" are absent.

This is why Desmond Tutu and Nelson Mandela refused to adopt the Nuremberg model of redressing the violated rights based on "retributive justice". They invoked the tribal tradition of ubuntu with its emphasis on "restorative justice" based on co-responsibility leading to confession and reconciliation. The criminals could not get away with murder, as some critics of the Truth Commission feared. The perpetrators of injustice were called to book, not in order to be harassed, but to be healed by an offer of forgiveness in exchange for a frank confession of repentance.

The Jewish concept tikkun olam, the reparation or betterment of the world, is also a kind of reconstruction. There is a risk with excessive memory, where the past conditions the present, where Arafat becomes a new Hitler. Such excessive memory will empty Hitler of meaning and should make us reflect on the meaning of metaphors. One has to reckon with the fact that there is in the Jewish world sometimes an excessive paranoia, an excessive memory of the Shoah. There is an important verse in the Jewish tradition: "Therefore it shall be, when the Lord your God has given you rest from all your enemies around, in the land which the Lord your God gives you for an inheritance to possess, that you shall blot out the remembrance of Amalek from under heaven;" (Deut.25, 19). Remembering the danger of excessive memory, Jews should therefore remember Amalek but with great caution.

Is there a place for silence or amnesia in memory or how do we deal with excessive memory? One must be wary of simplistic metaphors, dividing the world into good or evil in too facile a way. One must realise that one sometimes has to consciously discontinue remembering. One must realise that there is a relationship between memory and idolatry. When you become a slave to your memory, there is a risk of becoming idolatrous. This is a challenge also in peace building: in the pursuit of peace, there is a danger in becoming overwhelmed by wrath and anger. Anger can become idolatry when you lose the face of the other.

The evaluation of the consultation was overwhelmingly positive. There were justified remarks, which were noted: a Palestinian presence might have added another important focus, which could have been a healthy reminder of the political dimension of what is said in the Jewish-Christian dialogue. Poverty should have been an issue in itself and as a challenge to our talk about shalom and ubuntu. Certain issues were not at all mentioned: secularisation, agnosticism, Islam.

The message from Yaoundé captures in telegraphic style some of the vital points of the consultation and indicates a fervent wish that there is some kind of continuation to this kind of Jewish-Christian dialogue. While one may think that we have said what is to be said in the Jewish-Christian dialogue and time now has come for us to assess in an intra-Christian/intra-Jewish reflection the fruits of this dialogue, there are still both among Christians and among Jews refreshing and vital discoveries to be made of each other. It is maybe here that the WCC has a key role to play, providing a space for encounters that otherwise would never have happened.

Hans Hucko

The meaning and scope of *ubuntu*

Introduction

To enrich our reflections, which are already well-developed, on Jewish-Christian dialogue, we will explore here the concept of *ubuntu*. Several points will be articulated, beginning with the definition of *ubuntu*: what this concept means, particularly for certain cultures in the south of the African continent. Then we will see how the *ubuntu* concept is related to that of muoyo, which means life. This analysis will take us to other cultures within the Bantu family, so that we can appreciate the idea that *ubuntu*, to be well understood, must be seen within a community context. Finally we will make a connection between *muoyo* and *ntu*, to bring out the importance of the link between humankind and the rest of the creation. In conclusion we will show that the rules of *ubuntu*, which are no different from the rules of life, *muoyo*, are today being scorned, violated and neglected, which is contributing to large areas of conflicts in our societies.

Ubuntu: definition

An article by Muendanyi Mahamba[1] is a good place to start defining the concept of *ubuntu*. The term comes from the Zulu language, and the Setswana translation is *botho*. In Venda, the language of Muendanyi Mahamba, it is *vhuthu*. Mahamba says rightly that understanding this concept is a question not only of language, but also of culture. The basis, however, is the same. He writes:

> "Botho means 'our humanity'; it embraces everything which makes us human. *Botho* is essentially that which distinguishes humankind from the animal kingdom. But it means something more ... In the spirit of *ubuntu* or of *botho*, a person is supposed to play the role which belongs to him or her in the community. Individual behaviour is judged in accordance with the community's expectations, which it considers correct. For example, to describe someone by saying that 'Mpho has *ubuntu*' does not say enough. Yet in reality, the whole meaning is there. A person hearing these words soon understands that Mpho is a man full of love, who lives in such a way as to fulfil his social obligations. Mpho is conscious not only of his own rights, but also of his duties towards his neighbours. On the other hand, if one says 'Neo ga se motho' *(Neo does not have botho)*, it means that Neo is doubtless an unsociable person, a self-centred personality."[2]

When Mahamba applies his understanding of *ubuntu* to what we mean by democracy, he speaks of values such as justice, truth, respect, honesty and equality as its essential ingredients. Without these values, in his view, it is not possible to have a truly democratic society.

125

At a more practical level, another author, Mandla Gamede[3], presents the *ubuntu* concept from the viewpoint of community and humanitarian activity, in analysing the meaning of *ziklife*, which is both a cultural and an economic phenomenon, the aim of which is to reduce financial constraints in funeral practices. It motivated some citizens of a Johannesburg neighbourhood[4] to try to find a solution to this problem of costs. Thus their action is based on respect for the human person, that is, *ubuntu*. By joining together to found a sort of funerary cooperative, they put into practice their sense of humanity, their *ubuntu*, towards their fellow citizens, both those who had died and those still living who share the same love. In this way they were able to make burial services less costly, so that everyone can afford them. The respect for human dignity, love in practice, relief from the weight of economic constraints due to costly burials, demonstration of solidarity — all this constitutes the deeper meaning of *ubuntu*.

In an article entitled "What Apartheid Has Done to the African Family and Community and How the Present Situation Can Be Transformed"[5], Stanley Mogoba invites South African society to face the challenge of reviving the sense of being human, *ubuntu*, so as to succeed in repairing the damage caused by the effects of apartheid. He writes:

> "The greatest challenge in South Africa is how we should change people's hearts. We should teach them how to accept one another and how to live together in harmony. We should change the superiority and inferiority complexes they have. We should make human again our people who have been dehumanised — whites as well as blacks. We should revive the consciousness of blacks, the consciousness of whites and the national consciousness. By that I mean the sense of being human and proud of it. No more exclusiveness, but affirmation of ourselves and of one another. We need to revive ubuntu."

Mogoba continues:

> "*Ubuntu* means to love and take care of others, ubuntu means to be nice to others, ubuntu means to be welcoming, ubuntu means to be fair and understanding, ubuntu means to be filled with compassion, ubuntu means to help those who are in distress, ubuntu means to be frank and honest, ubuntu means to have good manners. A country which practises ubuntu is the closest on earth to the kingdom of God."

Ubuntu and *Muoyo*

To see properly the scope of the *ubuntu* concept, I have to turn to my own culture. The word *ubuntu*, as found in the Bantu family of languages, would mean "humanity" or "the fact of being human". In Chiluba[6] it is translated as *bumuntu* (*bu-* is a prefix indicating state or modality, and *-muntu* means person). *Muntu mulunze* means "man" and *Muntu mukaji* means "woman". *Bumuntu* is the quality which human beings have of expressing and affirming their being, their existence. This affirmation takes place through the sharing of life, *muoyo*, since to live or to enjoy one's life, for the Bantu, is to respect community norms and to promote the well-being of all, men, women and children.

In Chiluba, the term *muoyo* is used as a greeting, and greeting also has the sense of a blessing.[7] When one says *Muoyo, tatu* ("Good day, sir") or *Muoyo, mamu* ("Good day, ma'am"), one wishes the person long life, well-being, good health. Thus when *muoyo* is understood as a greeting and a blessing, it is close to the concept of *shalom*, which we shall speak about presently.

In the Bantu African concept of *muoyo*, the conditions of life in the present reflect the rhythm and the dynamism of *Muoyo* (with a capital M). What makes life pleasant and beneficial is to have good relations among human persons (*Bantu*) on one hand, and on the other between these persons and the rest of the universe. This interdependence constitutes the ontological basis necessary for a sort of "universal epistemology", which makes possible human knowledge as well as human existence and human development. In any case, to know a *muntu* implies neither separation from nor abstraction of the object which is known. The subject, in the act of knowing, senses or intuits a certain continuity between itself and the known object. For a thing is or exists when it participates in the dynamism of *Muoyo*. The "epistemological universality" consists in the subject and the object of knowing living in unity, for they are united in *Muoyo*. This is why even inanimate things are spoken of as being living or dead, which is not the same as animism. When a car breaks down, one says *mashini akufa* (in Chiluba) or *motuka ekufi* (in Lingala), that is, the car "is dead", its life, *muoyo*, is gone. One can say the same of a tree, a flower, a bottle or a serpent. The things which one is looking at or experiencing are of course different, but they are not separate from one another in *Muoyo*.

The coexistence of the living and the dead is another example. "The dead are not dead", said Birago Diop. The alternation of death (*lufu*) with life (*muoyo*) demonstrates to what extent the dead and the living are connected. If "the dead are not dead", it is because they have life (*muoyo*) in *Muoyo*. Death and life simply constitute the two aspects of the universal dynamic field of *Muoyo*. At birth one takes possession of *muoyo*, just as at death one takes possession of *lufu*. The first is the path of entry into this world — the visible world — while the second is the passage to the other, invisible world, the world "beyond". All this takes place within *Muoyo*.

Muoyo and *Ntu*

The typology of *Ntu*, as demonstrated by Alexis Kagame[8], is another way of understanding the concept of *muoyo*. According to Kagame, *-ntu* is, linguistically speaking, a root which requires a determining prefix, so as to point to one of the four specific categories of the Bantu universe, which are:

- *Mu-ntu*, for a human being; plural *Ba-ntu*;
- *Ki-ntu*, for a thing; plural *Bi-ntu*;
- *Ha-ntu*, for place or time;
- *Ku-ntu*, for modality.

Janheinz Jahn explains that *Ntu* is "a central point of thought, from which living and dead, real and imaginary, past and future, communicable and incommunicable, high and low are no longer thought of as contradictory concepts."[5] Thus, just like *Muoyo*, *Ntu* provides the common reality shared by plants, men and women, fire, air, water and everything that exists. In this sense, the "universal epistemology" consists of a total, that is, universal perception of the meaning of nature which, since it relates to the qualities of *Muoyo*, generates a series of images carrying meanings which are indispensable for the course of life, *muoyo*.[10]

From this discussion it is clear that *bumuntu (ubuntu)* is a term which affirms the unity of nature (creation), since all humankind shares in nature's life. At the ethical level, this affirmation needs to be put into action by seeking the well-being of all, including the natural environment in which our evolution takes place. In any case the meaning of *ubuntu* enables us to break the chains of discrimination, of violence and conflict, to practise neighbourly love and to work for the highest values of life.

Conclusion

Ubuntu *in the family*

In many ways, the practice of *ubuntu (bumuntu)* is being corrupted nowadays when it is confronted with western values. In traditional African society, parents took seriously their responsibility to pass on *bumuntu* during the socialisation of their children.[11] Their love, their compassion and the education which formed the child's character were aimed at the cohesion of the community, reinforcing the values which affirm and strengthen *muoyo*, such as dignity, justice, solidarity, respect for others, as well as love. Through respecting others, the child was permeated by the philosophy of community life, as John Mbiti expressed it: "I am because we are; because we are, therefore I am."[12] This philosophy was visible in the process of socialisation of youth, and consequently supported all the efforts of community members to provide them with the proper setting for their development. Today it is no longer so. Children are violated, abused and mistreated by those who are supposed to protect them. The growing numbers of children who live in the street, and of children who become mothers or soldiers, are a sad witness to this fact. All this reflects the decline of the rules of *ubuntu* in modern society.

Another consequence is manifested by violence within the family. Lack of mutual respect between married persons gives rise to incalculable abuses. Women particularly are victims of their husbands' violence, so that they become second-class persons. Domestic violence is lack of respect for the rules of *bumuntu*. Only respect for these principles can guarantee that married life goes smoothly.

The African palaver

In traditional African society, violation of the standards of *ubuntu* called for a *palaver* to be convened. [13] During this proceeding, all participants - men, women and children - had an equal right to speak. The way the *palaver* was conducted expressed the very rhythm of *Muoyo*, and of course, of *ubuntu*. Respect between persons was observed. Even if it sometimes happened that insults or blows were exchanged, the *palaver* ended by sanctioning repentance, peace and understanding, and was followed by a community meal. [14] The aim was liberation, healing, the re-establishment of the social equilibrium, in short, *ubuntu*.

Inter-ethnic wars or conflicts

In recent decades we have seen wars and conflicts in Africa between different ethnic groups who, in principle, had lived together for centuries without problems. It would seem that rejection of or forgetting the values of *ubuntu*, which had been the foundation for human relationships between different ethnic groups, is the sources of these intolerable crises. The revival of these values would no doubt make it possible to rebuild the solid and sustainable basis for community life on which peace-making between peoples depends.

Kasonga wa Kasonga

NOTES

[1] Muendanyi Mahamba, "*Ubuntu* and Democracy", in *Challenge, Church and People*, No. 16, June-July 1993, 6-7.

[2] Mahamba, *op.cit.*, p. 7. (provisional English retranslation from the French)

[3] Mandla Gamede, "*Ubuntu* in Burial Societies", in *Challenge, Church and People*, No. 45, December 1997-January 1998, 26-27.

[4] This association is called *Zikhuliseni, Ziklife and Ziknews*. Address: Methodist House, 114 Rissik Street, P.O.B. 32610, Braamfontein 2017, Johannesburg, South Africa.

[5] "What Apartheid Has Done to the African Family and Community and How the Present Situation Can Be Transformed", in *Trinity Journal of Church and Theology*, Vol. VIII, September 1998 (Special Edition), 38 (provisional English retranslation from the French).

[6] Chiluba is the language spoken by the Luba peoples, who extend from Eastern and Western Kasai Provinces to Katanga in the Democratic Republic of Congo (former ZaVre).

[7] Kasonga wa Kasonga, *Toward Revisioning Christian Education in Africa: a Critical Reinterpretation of Hope and Imagination in Light of African Understanding of Muoyo*, doctoral dissertation. Princeton (USA): Princeton Theological Seminary, 1988, 82ff.

[8] Alexis Kagame, *La philosophie Bantu-Rwandaise de l'Etre*. Brussels: Académie Royale des Sciences d'Outre-Mer, 1956.

[9] Janheinz Jahn, *Muntu*. London: Faber & Faber, 1961, 101 (provisional English retranslation from the French).

[10] The images which make up African symbolism constitute a language expressing the profound drama of human life. They help people in their self-realisation. R.P. Mveng explains this phenomenon in these terms: "It would be an error to think that all the African symbols taken together constitute a sort of code, arbitrarily established according to the needs of a closed aesthetic system. Symbolism is language. As such, it expresses the reality of the universe conceived as a humanised world, as a life in which the fates of human beings and of things are created interactively. But symbolism is not just any language. It seeks to express the drama of life, of this gigantic struggle in which life and death are adversaries, constituting the dialectic basis of existence. And this struggle is only a prelude to victory, the victory of Life over Death." R.P. Mveng, *L'art de l'Afrique noire*, Mame, 1965, quoted by Louis-V. Thomas and René Luneau in *La terre africaine et ses religions*. Paris: Larousse, 1975, 111.

[11] Pierre de Quirini, *Des lois pour les jeunes*. Kinshasa: CEPAS, 1987, 56. "Traditional societies required great physical and moral qualities of their adult members. To become a full member of the clan, one had to be able to respond to all the demands of the rough life of an agrarian society. An adult man was expected to resist pain and be courageous in the hunt and in war. Adults were supposed to acquire all traditional knowledge about their ancestors, the wisdom they transmitted, knowledge of plants and animals. They were expected to know the techniques of building a house, of making tools, traps and dugout canoes. And in particular they were supposed to be capable of raising a family and defending it against all dangers."

[12] J.S. Mbiti, *African Religions and Philosophy*. London: Heinmann, 1969, 108-109 (provisional English retranslation from French).

[13] "Palaver" refers to a forum, a meeting of the family or clan, which was convened when a crisis occurred in the community (illness, the unexpected death of a child, robbery, rape, adultery etc.). It could take the form of a court.

[14] For more information on the *palaver*, see my article "African Christian Palaver: a contemporary way of healing communal conflicts and crises", in Emmanual Lartey, Daisy Nwachuku and Kasonga wa Kasonga, *The Church and Healing: Echoes from Africa*. Frankfurt/Main: Peter Lang (African Pastoral Studies), 1994, 49-65.

Shalom in Hebrew

The word for peace in Hebrew is shalom. It comes from the root SHLM, which means "wholeness", but also, "to pay one's debts". Thus we hear in it that to attain the blissful condition of wholeness, one must pay one's debts. People do not seem to be able to live in peace unless they learn to pay what they owe. They are on the brink of torment, consciously or unconsciously, within themselves as well as in their social relations.

If the Hebrew language has revealed to us that the issue of debt is central to establishing peace, we still have to answer the following questions:

- What debt are we talking about?
- In what areas is the debt owed?
- To whom do we owe this debt?
- And especially, how shall we pay the debt, after we have determined the amount?
- From whom have I borrowed, without paying back what I owed?
- What gifts are involved?

I have received as gifts:

- life,
- language,
- the earth, the garden that nourishes me,
- the law.

These four fundamental gifts have come to me from four sources:

- the Creator,
- my parents and ancestors,
- my teachers and those who have told me stories,
- the judges and legislators of my country.

Each of us was conceived through an act of love between two persons, to whom we owe our lives, in whatever way this act of love took place. The fifth of the *Ten Commandments* says clearly: "Honour your father and your mother, so that your days may be long in the land that the Lord your God is giving you."

This central commandment of the ten is in fifth place, and it is the only one which specifies a reward. Longer life is offered in exchange for protection and respect for those who gave us life. If they can live in peace, we too shall live in peace. The torment and difficulty of living comes from the lack of respect for those who have given you life. The couches of psychoanalysts continually bear witness to the painful symptoms which have been planted in people's lives because their personal accounts are loaded down with guilt.

But how does one repay such a debt?

The wise writers of our *Talmud* propose two royal roads to repayment of what we owe our parents. The first concerns their old age, the time of their lives when they need support, comfort and often help from us. When they are old, we become their protectors, as they were ours when we were children. They were the shield protecting our first steps in life, and we become the guardians protecting their last steps. Thus a child entering this world finds tranquillity in the sheltering arms of its parents, and parents who have become feeble with age find serenity in their children's protection. How many misunderstandings and bitter feelings of hatred and resentment we could spare ourselves if these attitudes of protection and respect were preserved between parents and children! How much conflict, frustration, violence and war could be avoided by a proper understanding between the generations, when they take the gamble of protecting life!

Does the thread which connects wholeness with the payment of debts, leading to peace, pass through the eye of the needle into life?

The second road proposed to us, to deliver ourselves from the burden of debt owed to those who gave us life, is a more general one having to do with daily life. In the same way as I received the gift of life, I can repay it by becoming a parent myself and giving life to children whom I myself bring into the world. The same virtues which were present, protecting my own life, can now be employed to my credit through my own life actions. Generosity and patience, which are absolutely necessary in establishing peace among human beings, reach their highest expression in the relationship between parents and their young child. The movements in Israel which are seeking to work out peace between its two peoples, Palestinian and Israeli, often use in their titles the word *savlanut*, which means "tolerance" in Hebrew, in the sense of patience. How can peace be made between two peoples if they cannot listen patiently to one another, in order to hear and understand one another's stories and the mysteries of one another's identity?

In one of the projects we are directing in Israel to enable meetings between Palestinian and Israeli youth, which is rightly called "Tolerance Village", we invite each community to speak its own language at meetings. The French young people participate in French, the Palestinians in Arabic and the Israelis in Hebrew. The time it takes to listen and to translate each intervention from one language into the other two creates a climate of mutual patience and respect which is precious for the quality of relationships. Patience is the noblest of soils, in which the trees of life and the fruits of peace can grow.

Our debt to our Creator is clearly more complex, because it presupposes that we first recognise how to name, and where to find, the

Creator. It is a great temptation to decide, on the basis of what we can see, that no one is there to whom we owe anything in regard to nature, life's garden which receives us and where we find nourishment. It is easy to conclude and to decree that the garden is left to us, that we are the "sole proprietors". Only a few ancient texts testify to encounters between selected persons and the Creator, under certain exceptional circumstances. But to what extent should we credit these testimonies, since they can easily be classified as the products of imagination, that source of consoling fantasies and embellishing myths for humanity in distress? Can these stories stand up to the categorical judgments of reason, the teacher of truth? The Hebrew tradition teaches us that we should eat each fruit and each product of the earth only after saying a particular blessing to remind us permanently of where it came from. It is so easy to forget that we have to protect ourselves against it.

Every 50 years in the land of Israel, at *Yovel* (Jubilee) time, we are even obliged to return the deed to land which we own, where we live, to its original owner. All the texts invite us to consider the fact that we are only passing through this land - we are nomads, passing on from one generation to the next the torch which lights humanity's march. The biblical commandments are organised as a process of perpetually being reminded of the debt which binds us to the Creator of heaven and earth. To forget the name of the creditor, to ignore this claim on us, can open a yawning gap which lets the gusts of human pride and desire for domination come rushing in, to the detriment of our neighbours. The axe of war is uncovered at the foot of the tree where the serpent appears to Eve, to hold out to her the prospect that she and Adam will be "like their Creator", after eating the fruit without remembering the voice or applying the word which they have heard.

The third gift which we receive is that of language. Every word we use has been forged and reworked by generation after generation. All together they constitute a treasure which we have inherited, and we do it so naturally that we often neglect to cite our sources when we have made the effort to recognise them. The Hebrew language is especially sensitive to this search for roots. Its constitution and rules which set the language in motion are always careful to start by finding the root of a word so as to understand it better. Pirkeh Avot's treatise on the Talmud, *The Maxims of the Fathers*, invites us never to forget to name our teachers from whom we have received this or that teaching. They promise us that on the day when we accomplish this exercise perfectly, the messianic era will dawn upon our battle lines, with its promises of calming human relations and bringing peace.

When we find ourselves quoting a text or a word without mentioning the person who said it or wrote it, we can set in motion an uneasiness, provoke resentment or even open a conflict. The way to regain the peace which has been lost is usually very simple; we can make amends by naming the name which we have omitted. Language is not only subject to acknowledging its parentage and naming its ancestors; it cannot be appropriated by the "I" of the one who is speaking without referring to his or her "teacher", in thinking the truth of the teacher's wisdom and reasoning.

We have all experienced scenes in which language is twisted, becomes duplicitous or disguises itself, and where anger, fury and contempt rise in the veins of the person who feels duped, betrayed, rejected or humiliated by the person who is lying. The debt which is ours in speaking our language is twofold. The one is that of citing our sources and other persons to whom we are referring, and the other compels us to recognise the presence of the other person as an attribute of truth. This twofold debt is always present in every use of language which brings us together with other persons. Not to respect it is to take the risk, at any moment, of turning our steps toward misunderstanding and war.

The African "palaver" is a profound way of setting in motion this peace-making power of words. It allows each person to speak and be heard in his or her own name, while the group pursues a common quest: to abolish the conflict, through a shared search for the truth.

Finally, the fourth debt which we have mentioned brings us to recognise from whom we have received the law; to whom do we owe this debt? In the three monotheistic religions, the law has been transmitted to us by prophets who themselves received it from the Creator, each prophet on the basis of his particular kind of relationship with God. Moses, Jesus and Mohammed, each in his own place and time, have been the fundamental mediators of a relationship between humankind and the its Creator. Three facets of the same revelation of the law: "You shall not kill, you shall not steal, you shall love your neighbour as yourself."

To forget to pay one's debt in regard to the source of the law is to leave an empty space in the human conscience, and this could be taken over by Nimrod's Tower of Babel, by the perversities of Sodom and Gomorrah, by the Pharaohs of Egypt. Of course, the priests and kings who claim to have taken their laws from the great revealed texts can also subject the law to their needs and "enslave" it in their own service. Even so, any attentive reader of the revealed text will find there the divine will expressing the desire to encounter a human being directly, who can carry God's law in freedom and responsibility. The law brought to us through the voices of the prophets aims to free us from the yokes of dictators, paranoid leaders and false messiahs. By citing or invoking the source of the law, by paying our debt to it, we humans are enabled to come together in freedom and equality before it. The proposals of philosophers and ideologists who have preferred to see the law as rooted in the supreme principle of reason rather than that of revelation still achieved the same effects. They were opposing the same tyrants as we are, and their list also includes the fanatics, "God's crazies", the integrationists in every camp who refuse to separate religion from the state, the sacred from the profane.

It would still require a difficult debate to determine which of the two authorities, revelation or reason, is the most exacting in bringing human beings to pay their debt to the source of the law. Reason demands that subjectivity be sacrificed to ensure that reason is maintained inviolate for everyone, in the general interest. But isn't this a heavier sacrifice for the individual than the demand for submission to the law according to the Creator's word, transmitted by the prophets? Are the surrenders and the frustrations of human beings in "paying tribute to civilisation", as Sigmund Freud defines them in his book *Civilisation and its Discontents*, more likely to re-emerge from repression in the civilisation of reason, or in that of revelation? Which is the better guardian against these left-overs, these failures to attain absolute power - to "enjoy" it, in Jacques Lacan's sense - that are in danger of breaking out as destructive powers, as devastating death wishes? I am simply afraid that this peace, which would seem to be the reward for paying our debts, is encountering powerful obstacles in our modern age — ferocious, unconscious opposition forces which lie concealed in the depths of what we have forgotten. We are meeting here, you and I, all children of Abraham, educators, priests, militants, believers and idealists in a world-wide society, a global village which grows more and more opaque and rebellious.

We owe it to one another to keep the lights of a Word burning in our daily encounters with one another and with others, against the winds and the tides of hate and indifference, against war. This task will demand a great deal of us. Meetings between peoples are just so many precious sources of new energies, given to us to keep us in our covenant with the words of our prophets. The spirit of listening, of respect and love for one's neighbour, are just so many pillars of the peace which lives among us, that is, as we say in Hebrew, the name of the Creator and supreme mediator of life between human beings.

Peace is the holy name

In the Hebrew tradition the name of the Creator may not be pronounced, or represented in any way. The only knowledge which we may have consists in words which characterise, such as *Truth, Justice* and *Peace* — these three are fundamental. The city which is privileged to be the holy dwelling place is Jerusalem, in Hebrew *Yerushalaim*, which is generally translated "city of peace"; *ir* means "city", and *shalom*, plural *shalaim*, means "peace". The building of the Temple in Jerusalem was not granted to King David, who had conquered the city. According to the book of Samuel, the prophet Nathan reveals that the king had spilled too much blood, so the Creator did not allow him to build the temple which was to receive the holy name of Peace. The conqueror had the glory of composing, for the holy name, the hymns of the Presence, the Psalms, but not the dwelling place for the holy name. The man of war could nurture enthusiasm and hope through his words, but could not build the house of humanity, designed to be characterised by peace. His son's name, Solomon, *Shlomo* in Hebrew, comes from the root *shalom*, peace; it was he who was charged with building the Temple in Jerusalem. During the forty years of his reign he managed to keep the peace, both among his people and between them and other nations.

The sages of the *Talmud* were so concerned to teach us the importance of peace in directing the building of the Temple that they tell us that no iron tools were allowed in the work, since they recalled weapons of war. But how could the blocks of stone be shaped? One might well ask. It turns out there was a sort of insect, the *shamir*, which gnawed the stone the way termites chew through wood.

The sacrifices offered in the Temple were intended to calm the violence and anger which go with guilt feelings in human beings, and to allow people to "atone" for their faults. The sacrifice intervened to "pay their debts" to the law against which they had transgressed. It took place at the altar, with the help of the *cohanim*, the priests, in front of the Holy of Holies where the tablets of the law were kept, which had been received on Mount Sinai and brought by Moses' people to Mount Sion in Jerusalem. The priests themselves were the heirs of Moses' brother Aaron, of whom it was said, *Ohev shalom verodef shalom*, *"he loves peace and he pursues peace"*. There are *midrashim*, commentaries which tell of the strategies which Aaron knew how to use to restore peace among the people, whenever it had been lost or was in danger. If two men were angry with one another, Aaron went to see one and said, "You know, I've just seen your friend. He's been quite unhappy since you've been at odds." Then he went to the other one and told him the same thing, how his friend was sad, and sorry to have been angry with him. Then when the two friends met in the street, their faces relaxed, they went to meet each other again, embraced and were back on the path of peace.

How often, in our role as teachers, we find ourselves pursuing this word of mediation between people steeped in hatred, so that they can own the Word and implement it once again, understand and forgive one another. At *Yom Kippur*, the "feast of the Great Pardon", which at the time of the Temple was led by the *cohahim*, the fundamental task is a threefold reconciliation, remembering and confessing our faults:

between a human being and God,

between a human being and his or her conscience,

between one human being and another.

According to the custom, during the ten days leading up to the festival everyone tries to go and see persons with whom they have fallen out and to be reconciled with them, preferably in the presence of witnesses, by asking their forgiveness for the mistakes, hurts and misunderstandings which have broken their relationship. Some people agree that of the three kinds of reconciliation to be obtained during this festival, the one which consists in forgiveness between oneself and one's neighbour is the most important task.

Jerusalem, city of peace

A commentary teaches us that the rock on which the Temple in Jerusalem was built was the site of the most dramatic actions of humankind according to the biblical account. Here on this rock Cain killed his brother Abel, and Abraham, at the Creator's command, brought his son Isaac here to sacrifice him, until God intervened again to save him. On this same rock Jacob fell asleep, weary from his journey, and dreamed of a ladder with angels ascending and descending between heaven and earth. A *midrash* teaches us that the field where this rock was, was chosen by Solomon, telling the uplifting story of two brothers who had lost their father and each received an equal share of inheritance from him. One of them, the father of several children, said to himself, "Why do I need all this money? I have the greatest riches of all, my children; my brother is alone, he needs this money much more than I do." He put his share of the inheritance in a bag to bring it secretly, at night, to his brother's house. Meanwhile, at the other side of the field, the brother who lived alone was thinking, "Why do I need all this money? My brother with all his children has many more expenses than I do." He, too, put his money in a bag and went out in the middle of the night to put it secretly in his brother's house.

At the spot where these two brothers met at night with their bags full, the Temple was built. It was built at the place where generosity and brotherly love redeemed Cain's frightful crime against Abel. It is the same place where the Creator tested Abraham's fatherhood, and announced to him that infanticide was no longer an acceptable sacrifice in the worship of God.

Thus the Temple in Jerusalem is dedicated as a place which welcomes generosity, love, justice, the foundation of a space for peace. Jerusalem is the city of these promises, which are fourfold:

- between heaven and earth there is no break, but a continuity, a prolongation, steps which symbolise Jacob's ladder;
- between brothers and sisters, life is lived together in generosity and the concern of each for the other: "I am my brother's/sister's keeper";
- between parent and child, the potential rivalry, the imagined murder can be sublimated in the respect for life;
- between humankind and the Creator we can put in place a relation, like a couple with their house, a civilisation, a humanity dwelling one with another, and say that the three modes of a human being are life, love and peace.

With the rebirth of Israel, the name of Jerusalem resounds once more among the nations. Abandoned as a capital by the nations for almost two thousand years, while the Jewish people were in exile, it has taken its place, its dignity and its *raison d'être* once again, by becoming the chosen capital of the Hebrew people. The re-awakening of Jerusalem, after two thousand years of hibernation during which it was de-baptised, destroyed, abandoned, is certainly painful. Once again at the centre of human memory and of the network of associations with the monotheistic religions, Jerusalem shakes our consciences. Once again it is beautiful, coveted, the subject of envy and jealousy. Beautiful Jerusalem turns the heads of the nations, sometimes to the point of madness.

During the Oslo peace process, up to its last stage at Camp David in July 2000, the warring parties concerned were almost able to formulate solutions for sharing, between the two peoples, the land, the water, power, and two states, Palestine and Israel. But Jerusalem, city of peace, became the touchstone for the most difficult disagreements to resolve, and the voice of Cain resounded again over its face. How was this city to be shared which is the house, the dwelling place, the name of the holy? How could the sovereignty of the holy be respected, and the three monotheistic revelations be restored to their successive places and the dignity of each? How to avoid the father sacrificing his son and the sons making a pact to sacrifice the father? Every one of us is called upon to resolve these questions, and it is the equilibrium and the peace of humankind which is at stake. A mishandling of these questions raised by Jerusalem will become the danger of war in the Middle East which, in the current context, could take on the aspect of a new world war. But if we meet together to love peace, to think about peace, across our different traditions, the task of all our clergy will become the echo of Aaron's credo: "Love peace and pursue peace." To protect Jerusalem from pride and covetousness is a task laid upon us, so that peace may dwell among us in each of our houses.

When he came out of the Ark, Noah sent a dove to find out whether life had returned to the earth. It came back with an olive branch in its beak. The symbols of the olive tree and the dove were to become symbols of peace for all nations. Peace is inseparable from the love of life, from protecting it and from the song of hope which spurs it on. A rainbow became the new sign of the covenant between the Creator and humankind: the Creator promised never again to destroy human life, as had been done during the flood, when the Creator was angry. The rainbow tells about this marvellous covenant founded on plurality. Every colour has its place, and every branch of the human race its path, but they are all bound together in their singularity and plurality. The interface where the rainbow appears, between rain and sun, water and fire, diffracts the ray of light without causing it to lose its unity. Jean Danielou invites us to listen to the resonance of this process: "As the soul goes nearer to the light it becomes more beautiful, and in the light it takes on the shape of a dove."

Conclusion

We have gathered at Yaoundé to analyse and discern what are the tools and the attitudes which can make us "peace-builders". The dignity of humankind, represented in the *ubuntu*, the African palaver, and the way it is mediated which shows the African love of life, are guaranteed ways of walking this path, not dispersed and divided but reunited in the colours of the rainbow. If the Hebrew *shalom* turns us toward the state of wholeness which is present when one has paid one's debts, the teaching of esteem which replaced the teaching of contempt after the Nazi catastrophe in Europe is also very much a part of this revolution. There where Cain murdered his brother Abel, we can follow in Solomon's footsteps and rebuild the house of peace. The love which is present in the *Song of Solomon*, between Solomon the Hebrew and the black Ethiopian Queen of Sheba, remains the rock of our hope.

Henri Cohen-Solal

Memories and experiences of violence

Introduction

The subject on which I have been asked to reflect takes me back to situations which I have experienced over more than 40 years. As perhaps some of you know, I come from Rwanda, that little country in the centre of Africa, the source of horrors and images of death which have deeply shocked the world, especially during the genocide of 1994, the climax of over 40 years of repeated violence.

I had the misfortune or the opportunity, as an eyewitness, to belong to a generation which saw the birth and development of an ideology of hate, hate which culminated in the physical elimination of over a million persons in a three-month period. Those who think Africans are not capable of organising things minutely and efficiently are mistaken. If the genius, creativity and tenacity which my fellow citizens showed in the service of death could be turned towards serving life, our country, our continent and even the world would be profoundly changed. It is not my intention here to analyse the causes and consequences of the Rwandan genocide. Those who want to know more about it can benefit from the lucid analysis by Dr. Tharcisse Gatwa which has just been published by Clé & Haho.

I have decided to make my personal experiences the basis for a more comprehensive reflection.

Tensions between remembering and forgetting

The undermining of certainties and convictions

Rwandans are often asked to explain how what happened could be possible. This question is terribly embarrassing for us, because we were as surprised as everyone else, even though we had witnessed the rapid increase of tensions and the process of propaganda. We could never have imagined that human barbarism could grow to the proportions which it did in our country.

At the time of the 1994 genocide, I was in Nairobi, Kenya, working for the All African Conference of Churches. Due to my work in its Department of Theology and Interreligious Dialogue, of which I was in charge, I was able to propose that African theology move from the paradigm of liberation to one of reconstruction, a paradigm which is known by this name today. I still believe today that the reconstruction of Africa is possible, by making use of all the human and material potential which God has given us. We were overwhelmed and disoriented when the intelligence and genius which we were counting on were used in the service of evil and of death, bringing the tragedy of genocide to my own country.

During these years of study and work in Rwanda, in Europe or in Kenya, I had been so proud of African culture and values as centred on the *Ubuntu* concept, that is, the sacred character of life, that my lengthy intellectual development and the certainties which governed my life and my commitments were profoundly shaken. This shock left my mind in a state of reappraisal from which I have not yet fully recovered, moreover, and with which I returned to Rwanda in 1995 to take up the task of reconstructing the church and our society which had become profoundly disintegrated.

During the synod meeting in February 1995 at which I was elected president of the Presbyterian Church in Rwanda, my fears were heightened when a colleague and pastor pointed out that my election as head of a shattered church in a devastated country gave me an excellent opportunity to put into practice the theology of reconstruction about which I was so good at theorising.

Dry bones

As I faced this huge challenge, a Bible text renewed my spirit and became a profound source for my inspiration and commitment.

"The hand of the Lord came upon me, and he brought me out by the Spirit of the Lord and set me down in the middle of a valley; it was full of bones. He led me all round them ... and they were very dry. He said to me, 'Mortal, can these bones live? I answered, 'O Lord God, you know.' Then he said to me, 'Prophesy to these bones, and say to them: O dry bones, hear the word of the Lord. Thus says the Lord God to these bones: I will cause breath to enter you, and you shall live. I will lay sinews upon you, and will cause flesh to come upon you, and cover you with skin, and put breath in you, and you shall live ; and you shall know that I am the Lord.' " (Ezekiel 37:1-6)

The cause of Rwanda's suffering lies not only in the vastness of the crimes committed by Rwandans against other Rwandans. It is amplified by the fact that the survivors of the massacre, both butchers and victims, have to learn to live together and to share everything. This is the inevitable reality which we come up against with our much-discussed reconstruction. On the one hand are the people who long with all their hearts to forget, in order to go on living; on the other are those who are convinced that to forget would be a further crime, which would never be forgiven them.

In fact the people who saw members of their own family kill neighbours with whom they had lived together for years are suffering terribly under the weight of guilt by implication, and the images of the scenes which took place before their eyes. They were witnesses to murders, and they know where these people were hastily buried; to ask them to speak about this would mean asking them to accept this burden of shame and the consequences of the crimes which were committed. These traumatising feelings were made worse by the attitude or even deliberate willingness of a few unscrupulous people to profit from the weakness of others, to humiliate them or to take things from them.

On the other hand there were and continue to be those who escaped the genocide, or members of exterminated families who had just returned from exile and wanted to know the circumstances of their loved one's deaths, and in cases where they had been hastily shovelled into mass graves, to bury them with dignity. The former wanted to forget everything, while the others wanted to know everything and preserve the remembrance at any cost.

To tell the truth, there has never been an open debate on this subject. Such a debate, moreover, would not have been possible in view of the tensions, traumas and uncertainties of the period immediately following the genocide.

There were many initiatives all over the country to exhume the bodies and organise ceremonies of mourning and burial. The churches themselves seemed to be divided on this issue. Some, following the example of the Presbyterian Church of Rwanda, of which I had just been elected president, were convinced that any possible reconstruction of the torn fabric of Rwandan society absolutely had to begin with this act of honouring the victims and giving them an appropriate burial. Others preferred to speak directly of forgiveness and reconciliation, which made those who had escaped feel guilty, since they would inevitably be chastised if they were not able to forgive unconditionally, following Christ's example.

I shall never forget the extreme tension which we had to deal with when we organised the burial, at Remera, of six of our 16 pastors who had been killed during the genocide. A large part of our constituency was expressing resistance to the very principle of exhuming the bodies in order to bury them again with dignity. In fact, a delegation of Christians came to see me in my office, Bibles in hand, to ask me on what basis we could follow blindly the initiative of the government, since this was liable to lead us into the anti-Protestant heresy of praying for the dead. I was very happy to receive this delegation, since they were daring to say out loud what many others were whispering. But in a way I was theologically unprepared, since for almost a year I had been dealing with emergencies every day without necessarily drawing theological and doctrinal conclusions as the basis of my involvements. Before the discussions could go further, one of my colleagues, a survivor who was present, suggested we read the following text:

"David went and took the bones of Saul and the bones of his son Jonathan from the people of Jabesh-Gilead, who had stolen them from the public square of Beth-shan, where the Philistines had hung them up, on the day the Philistines killed Saul on Gilboa. He brought up from there the bones of Saul and the bones of his son Jonathan; and they gathered the bones of those who had been impaled. They buried the bones of Saul and of his son Jonathan in the land of Benjamin in Zela, in the tomb of his father Kish; they did all that

the king commanded. After that, God heeded supplications for the land."
(2 Samuel 21:12-14)

The reading of this passage, which we also used everywhere else, clarified the situation and the process continued without further antagonism. Today almost 100 genocide sites have been identified in different corners of the country, although much remains to be done to construct and organise them properly. In addition, the command to forget in order to forgive has lost the impetus which certain superficial preachers were trying to give it.

A major challenge remains: how to preserve the remembrance, while at the same time developing the psychological and spiritual motivation on which forgiveness and reconciliation can be built?

Remembrance and violence in African theology

Remembrance as the basis of Christianity

Christianity is a religion founded on remembrance. Whether we speak of the different references or liturgical celebrations, the memory of the essential facts of the Christian faith inspires comprehension and experience of them for successive generations of Christian believers. This process of familiarisation with the symbols or rites extends to believers' making them their own, to an astonishing degree. The most eloquent example of this is the cross. We all know what is represented by this symbol of atrocious and shameful death. But today the cross is proudly worn by the high dignitaries of Christian churches. The evocation of the life, death and resurrection of Christ is not only part of our language, but also of our sacraments and the entire life of the Christian church.

In other words, the integration of the experience of violence into the individual or collective memory of Christians takes place in obedience to the principles of Christ's love, who showed, through his life and through his death, a way of responding to violence. "Father, forgive them, for they do not know what they are doing." (Luke 23:34)

This love beyond measure for a human being whom we also recognise as our brother or sister becomes our reference point and inspiration in managing the memories and the experience of violence. Thus we reach the point where we can respect and preserve memories, so that we can draw lessons from them for the future and through them can envisage prospects for rebuilding peace - a peace founded on mutual recognition and respect, not on impunity and lack of redress for injustice.

Preserving remembrance leads us to recognise the seriousness of the crimes which have been committed and should allow us to conceive, together, mechanisms for re-establishing the truth. Recognising the seriousness of crimes would make it possible for us to arrive at commitments to prevent it, so that no such thing could happen ever again.

In its effort at self-affirmation and the healing of memories, African theology takes very seriously the extraordinary and privileged relations which exist between Jews and Africans. In this perspective, the important thing is not to remember the time of slavery in Egypt; it would be a betrayal of remembrance to recall only this unhappy experience and forget that Africa proved its great open-mindedness by welcoming Joseph and his family and entrusting major responsibilities to him. Furthermore, the fact that the Hebrew people spent 400 years on the African continent is a sufficient explanation for the cultural and spiritual similarities between our two peoples, for example in the concepts of *Shalom* and *Ubuntu*. We also know that long before this experience of living and sharing together, there was a blood relationship between the two peoples which was expressed in Moses' marriage to a Cushite woman, a black African woman who insisted on the importance of circumcision.

At the birth of Christianity, Africa was not absent either. Some people tend to think that this continent has only existed since the age when they themselves claim to have discovered it, and that Christianity is only a few hundred years old in Africa. But among the visitors to Jerusalem who were amazed at the Pentecost event, some were Africans. The church has never stopped developing on this continent, so that in the 4th century African Christians constituted 20 per cent of Christianity. Furthermore, collective remembrance always recalls the role of the eminent African theologians Tertullian and Augustine, whose work left its mark on the early centuries of the church.

From liberation to recognition

Let us also recall why it was so necessary for African theology to make the transition from the liberation paradigm to that of reconstruction in the early 1990s. The liberation paradigm was in fact utilised by the theology developed in Latin America and Africa, in parallel to the liberation movements in the countries under colonial occupation. This theological step was initially taken in reaction to all sorts of prejudices, which are still in circulation today, with regard to colonised peoples and their cultural values. When most of our countries had attained political independence, the liberation paradigm and the theological reaction began to lose their dynamism. Thus it became necessary to move to the reconstruction paradigm — centred essentially on the Books of Nehemiah and Ezra — while liberation theology drew its inspiration from its reading of the Book of Exodus.

One of the major challenges which we have is the prospect of a lasting peace founded on justice and equity. Our continent needs such perspectives, as does our world. Are we allowed to take our faith in God as a foundation which could make it possible to build a lasting peace, without falling into the temptation to erase or betray our memories? Pessimists find it difficult to accept this option, because religious co-existence is one of the time bombs which are in danger of generating conflicts and wars of great seriousness.

We dread all the consequences of what is going on today in Afghanistan with regard to fundamentalists who are in danger of becoming radicals. Nevertheless, on the basis of the African understanding of faith, it is inconceivable that human beings who respect God would fight in God's name. To fight in the name of God, according to the African concept of the Supreme Being, is to make of God an idol which needs to be protected by its creatures. Furthermore, respect for this God is only possible if one respects the harmony of relationships among the components of reality. This is certainly the perspective of the prophet Isaiah who invites us to dream of a world at peace:

"The wolf shall live with the lamb,
the leopard shall lie down with the kid,
the calf and the lion and the fatling together,
and a little child shall lead them.
The cow and the bear shall graze,
their young shall lie down together;
and the lion shall eat straw like the ox.
The nursing child shall play over the hole of the asp,
and the weaned child shall put its hand on the adder's den.
They will not hurt or destroy on all my holy mountain,
for the earth will be full of the knowledge of the Lord
as the waters cover the sea." (Isaiah 11:6-9)

From a Christian viewpoint, the ethical principles of love, of justice and peace are the values on which the gospel calls us to base our choices, our actions and our commitments. Nevertheless, the case of Rwanda calls into question the kind of Christianity which we are circulating here, since genocide was manifested in a country where more than 80 per cent of the population claims to be Christian. The critical reflection which we have conducted regarding Christianity in Rwanda leads us to be sorry that we drove out the traditional religion in which it was inconceivable to kill a woman, even during a war, since she is the carrier of fertility. However, we remain convinced that the Christian faith, properly understood, can bring us to construct a lasting peace.

Conclusion

After seven years of pursuing this path, the image which dominates my mental universe, with regard to the church and my country, is no longer that of dry bones. The bones have come together, the sinews have been restored and covered by the body. I can even say that a faint breath now animates this body which was formerly in decay. However, I am aware that we still have a long way to go in building together and caring for our remembrance, so that the unspeakable thing which we have experienced can never happen again, here or elsewhere. What I fear above all is that the world seems to be going on without really learning the lessons of collective remembrance. I often say to my African friends that what happened here could, unfortunately, happen elsewhere if some simple conditions came together: a population living mostly in poverty, a dictatorship afraid of being overthrown and the identification of some group or other as its emissary. However, today it does seem possible to learn a lesson from our past experiences, so as to look towards a future in which the next generations will be able to live in peace and dignity.

André Karamaga

The memory and experience of violence

This title reminds us, in case we have forgotten, that violence occupies two stages in time. First there is the time during which it unfurls itself seemingly without bounds, the time that belongs to History (with a big axe [homonym of "h" in French], as Georges Perec says), the time composed of victories and defeats, of barbarism and bravery, of lives cut down and lives saved. Then comes the time afterwards, which begins as soon as the violence is suspended, momentarily or for good, by a peace or a status quo - the time of memory, when nothing is left of the violence but its scars: the places, monuments, stories, photos and names which must be collected and reconstructed so that the living can go on living.

The first of these periods is short, but no less vivid: like a deep gash, it establishes a "before" and an "after" in both individual and collective life. The second can go on into all eternity. It is the revenge of the victims, while the authors of the violence do their best to push away and deny completely what they have done. When the era of reconciliation comes at last, the memories, which inevitably contradict one another, negotiate amongst themselves to decide what can and should be remembered and commemorated, so that when this first task is finished, that which can and should be forgotten is also given its due.

During both periods, that of history and that of memory, we all try to wall off from ourselves the senselessness of the contradiction between the triumph of peace as a heavenly idea and its defeat in the real world, its precariousness and fragility in the face of the world's dangers weighing upon it; or conversely, the contradiction between violence which is dreaded and condemned in the human mind and its actual hegemony in the arena of international relations. Why such a hiatus, such an abyss?

How does it happen, in fact, that peace, which we instinctively think of as good and take for granted as our goal, even more so during this consultation - how does it happen that peace only reigns over human relations with great difficulty and for the briefest of moments? If we are easily and unanimously convinced of the importance and the urgent necessity of peace, what lesson should we learn from the fact that so many nations and persons do not share our conviction and give themselves over, by choice or under compulsion, to the commerce of war? Why is peace only parenthetical in History, while religions and philosophies, both oral and written, are incessantly pleading for it? Should we think of violence as our common lot, to which we are condemned for the long term by history, or even by our human nature?

I do not pretend to be able to answer here these questions which arouse such uncertainty and horror at what the human race is capable of doing. It is enough that this question of the universality of violence, in every time and place, remains open in each one of us; that we keep going back to it as an obsession, which never lets us reach serenity, quiet, blessedness, despite all the promises of redemption that we all cling to in order to overcome the horror and ugliness of this world here below, and it is truly low and depressing. Let us beware of answering that all this is decided by our genes or by fate. I shall not pretend to offer you a vademecum, a guidebook to equip you with ideas and recommendations for ending violence. That would be presumptuous, and a hundred Nobel Peace Prize winners would soon admit how difficult it is. Even if violence is gaining ground and not being disarmed, we still have to pursue peace.

What I have to offer is therefore most of all a humble confession and an invitation to humility. But before making it, I would like to read you these lines from the French poet Charles Péguy, who has long been important to me. I often say these first lines over to myself, whenever I feel invaded by despair, when the hosts of war are marching shoulder to shoulder and mowing down the disunited and sparse forces of peace.

"No matter what we do, no matter what, they will always be ahead of us, they will always do more and accomplish more than we … It takes years and years to grow a human being. And after it has taken bread and more bread to feed him, and work and more work and more work, all sorts of work, it only takes one blow to kill a human being, one stroke with a sword and it's done. … To make a good Christian takes twenty years of ploughing. To unmake a good Christian, it's a minute's work with a sword. It's always like that. It's the nature of a plough to work for twenty years. It's the nature of a sword to work for one minute, and to accomplish more; to be the strongest; to finish the job. We, on the other hand, will always be the strongest, we will always go slower, we will always get less done. We are the team of those who build, and they are the team of those who demolish. We are the team of the plough, they are the team of the sword. We will always be beaten. They will always be on top, over and above us, no matter what we say."[1]

So let us, like Péguy, assume that violence reigns supreme, that it is that dreadfully efficient, works that quickly and that its effect is guaranteed. Let us assume that we are defeated by this asymmetrical structure. They are strong and we are weak, their task is easy and ours is hard. We have to take account of this painful truth that violence is victorious, not so as to give in to despair and bow before its omnipresence and its omnipotence, but to make sure that we are not wallowing in empty words which have no relation to reality. "No matter what we say."[2] What shall we think, what shall we say or imagine? This is the challenge for peace-builders.

Because violence is repugnant and revolting to us, we are tempted to ascribe it to the other person. It's always the other who is barbaric, always the other who has a monopoly on it. Let us be wary of these automatic reactions. People are born free and equal not only with regard to rights, but also with regard to choice. They can choose to do evil instead of good, to the extent that we can agree on a definition of these terms. Certainly there are social, economic and cultural inequalities, factors which are likely to make violence a possible option. But every time someone resorts to violence, there is an irreducible element of individual responsibility which cannot be legitimately obscured by any absolution, whether sociological or religious, nationalist or philosophical.

In this discussion of violence, of the experience and the memory which we have of it, I should like to divide my remarks into two parts. First I shall examine our relation to violence of which we ourselves are the authors, then our relation to violence of which we are the victims. Perhaps these two dimensions are two sides of the same coin; it seems that in the particular history of the Jewish people, and in that of Africans who endured the yoke of colonialism before they threw it off, the violence was endured first, before they had the means to exercise it themselves. Here we have a peculiarity of fate which, far from dividing us, could unite us. It could establish a sense of community around the experience and the memory of violence, out of an agreement to understand one another.

Violence and the sacred

The Jewish tradition ever since the Bible does not conceal the reality of violence in human relations. Far from considering it an exceptional phenomenon, the Bible provides an inventory of its multiple and varied forms and modalities. The judgment on principle which is brought against violence is dominated, above all justifications, explanations, excuses, legitimations and alibis of every kind, by the famous "You shall not kill" (Exodus 20:13). Laconic, general, directly addressed to the individual conscience, this commandment unconditionally condemns every threat which is raised against human life. This is the rule, this is the law, the word carved in stone which is the law of humanity. Everything else is literary, ornamental, casuistry and can be classified as exceptional. If, in positive terms, human beings are called to love our neighbour as ourselves, the commandment sets a limit beyond which we are forbidden to go: humankind may not violate the divine work of creation by murder. It is an even more peremptory affirmation when we consider that violence is inherent in the human condition. Furthermore, murder is not just the prerogative of two individuals or two peoples who don't know one another; it is fratricide, as the story of Cain and Abel reminds us.

If the end of time can be considered the point when peaceful relations will definitely be established among humans, historical time includes war in various forms. Rather than being excluded in principle, which would set the standard too high, war is subjected to rules and laws limiting its uses. Distinctions are made between optional and obligatory wars. War in itself is always less desirable than peace, but there are circumstances in which it is necessary. War is an expression of concrete human reality, but is not humanity's vocation; sometimes necessary, but never our inexorable destiny. An ambiguity clings to it when we turn from the human to the divine level and find God choosing to intervene in this way in historical reality. God's doing so, punishing the wicked, is not so much a demonstration that God is all-powerful as that God wants redress; justice cannot wait.

When the Jews went into exile, the question of whether to use force became a matter for purely theoretical speculation. Sages and rabbis could ramble on about the concept of just war, but since Jewish sovereignty was finished, taking such action was precluded. The Jewish people survived despite history and their ignorance of its mechanisms and instruments. History exposed them to blows and persecutions, but this political and military hibernation allowed them to keep their distance from every desire for power, every use of force, and from the consequences of such. Thus the break from the diaspora situation which Zionism represented encompassed the use of force as a possible option, and the criteria for using it.

Thinking about using force

The relationship with the use of force is, in fact, one of the most striking traits of the new identity and the new reality forged by the yishuv, the Jewish community reconstituted in Palestine. This issue hardly received any attention from their founding fathers, from Moses Hess through Pinsker to Herzl. They were too busy justifying the reasons for creating a homeland, in view of the plans of the Jewish diaspora, to imagine the problems which this homeland might create, including that of the use of force. Herzl had made an effort to define the political, diplomatic and economic conditions of re-emergence as a nation, but certainly not the eventuality of a conflict; had he foreseen this, it would surely have caused him distress or even despair, so far was it from his peaceful vision of the realisation of his plan. He had insisted enough on the legal character of the Jewish state to be created, and on its future neutrality, to be willing to devote the shortest paragraph of his work to this subject, and only the most trivial and conventional words: "a professional army (will be) equipped with all the modern means of war, to maintain internal and external order". What else could he have said, since his aim was to give Jews the possibility to "live as free people and to die in peace, in our own fatherland"?

But if there was no reflection on the use of force, it was because it did not seem that the question itself should be asked. Was not Zionism the final solution which was supposed to settle definitively the tensions between the Jews and the peoples amid which they had been living? Contrary to a later idea which ended up as the established view, the Jewish state as it was conceived did not intend to provide the persecuted people with the means of defending themselves against every potential enemy; it was expected to make the issue of resorting to force unnecessary, since this issue would have been resolved. By having gathered together in a land and having proclaimed their political sovereignty, they would be delivered once and for all from the profound cause of their insecurity, from the condition of their woes; being a minority. The root of all evil having been eradicated, every Jew could taste at last, after the tumult of living in the diaspora, the peace and joy of living amongst one's own people, at home in one's own land, the land flowing with milk and honey, "under their own vines and under their own fig trees" as the prophet Micah says (4:4). The stranger, the refugee, the well-named "wandering Jew" would be able to enjoy a native land and discover the serenity of those who possess the true key to happiness - the strength of quietness. Didn't this make it redundant to think of any other force in addition to the strength already obtained just by being at home, free and independent, out of reach of anti-Semitism from peoples or states?

It was the experience which the new immigrants brought to Palestine of having defended themselves against the pogroms in Russia, which was invoked in proposing, besides the ideal of Jewish labour, the duty for Jews to police themselves. Until now this had been the task of their Arab neighbours; now they made it their own business. For an unexpected ordeal awaited these thousands of Jews who had come mostly from Russia. Expecting to find their ancestral home desolate and abandoned, a "land without people", they found it inhabited. What was even more serious, they soon realised, was that they were still unwanted, just as they had been in Russia: a handful, a minority, watched by a suspicious majority. Incidents broke out, not as cruel as a pogrom but still striking innocent victims.

Was it the same identical situation? For many of them, yes; they believed that there is nothing new under the sun. What was different - an essential difference - was their reaction. Weak and powerless in Russia, they were less ready to fight because they did not feel at home there; weak and powerless in Palestine, they felt something within which called for them to react differently: not that again, never again, and especially not here in the land of Israel. The reason for this metamorphosis, which had already encouraged their will to defend themselves after Kishinev, was the decisive role played by what could be called a psychological preparation, a mental restructuring which affected the personalities of the pioneers. One could say their hearts were prepared, not so much in the way Ahad Ha'am had wished, but there was a willingness to prove themselves in this new land. This initiation was not concrete preparation for war, but it was a part of the remoulding of Jewish identity.

Since Zionism was not possible without a change in the Jewish personality, what values and models lent themselves to becoming part of it? In the Jews' view of themselves, as in the view of others, exile went hand in hand with weakness. The *galutic* stereotype of appropriate behaviour in exile, consisting of submission and powerlessness, sometimes to the point of caricature, was too common not to encourage the development of its antithesis. But stereotyped though it was, and although there were plenty of examples of the opposite in the diaspora, [3] this traditional image corresponded completely to the subaltern position of Jews in Western society. Returned to Zion to take back their freedom, their pride and independence along with their land, wouldn't the new immigrants who wanted to break with their past condition have begun logically to think of becoming strong men and women, in possession of all their physical powers? [4] But this strength mainly had to be used for the pioneering work on the land, confronting rebellious nature and the swamps infested with malaria.

But if, for someone like Gordon, the individual pioneer's willingness to work for the redeeming cause, the work on the land and the mystique of the effort which it demanded were sufficient to identify this metamorphosis, it was not the same for the leaders and the members of the first defence organisations, *Bar-Giora* in 1907 (named for the leader of the Jewish revolt against the Romans in 70 C.E.) and *Hashomer* in 1909 ("the guardian"). They did not see their role as strictly instrumental, and self-defence did not seem to them to be dictated only by insecure local conditions. This transformation was more than a tactical manoeuvre to gain respect. It was the sign that the diaspora mentality was gone for good, a sign that change had taken place: "it is a question of awakening in the hearts of the farmers and workers the feeling and the awareness that they alone are capable of defending themselves and protecting their goods … Our purpose is not temporary, the result of particular circumstances: it is a huge historical objective, a permanent one, with eternal value." [5] The two to three hundred people gathered there had an image of their mission as a revolutionary avant-garde, of necessity clandestine. Their approach did not shrink from embracing a certain mystique of power, using ancient Jewish symbols such as their rallying cry, from a poem by Ya'akov Cahan: "By fire and blood, Judah fell; by fire and blood, Judah will rise again."

Necessary evil or value in itself?

Whether as an end in itself or purely a means, in Zionist speeches the use of force leaned towards one or the other of two poles; it was seen both as a *necessity*, particularly for ensuring the policing of the new communes, and as a *value* emblematic of the new Jew; in other words, it was most often thought of, in a somewhat confused way, as a mixture of the two.

All speakers hark back to the pre-exilic era to legitimate the place ascribed to the use of force; from Gordon to Jabotinsky, from apostles of pacifism to military enthusiasts, everyone draws from the source of antiquity. But this harking back to the ancient past, to the time before the exile, does not restore the same images or generate the same values in all cases. For cultural Zionists, the restoration of a Jewish entity was to draw upon the spirit of the prophets and the universal values associated with them; the return of the Jews to Israel was to find its profound justification in the vow to build a just city, thus giving new hope to humanity. In the spirit of Ahad Ha'am, this spiritual homeland, giving light to all Jews and to the world, would only need to display the external signs of power. This would be a country like no other, not just one more new state on the map. Thus there was no need to think of the use of force as a value; the art of war belongs to Esau and not to Jacob. Since the will to renew Jewish identity and the concern to restore dignity to the people are legitimate, they should not lead to the loss of the Jewish uniqueness forged by morality and history, by the Bible and the Exile.

How should this new ethos be promoted, personal and collective dignity be regained, and self-mastery be recovered, while keeping it within bounds, so that legitimate defence did not become illegitimate defence? This is what worried Ahad Ha'am and his disciples. It was not possible to deny outright that there might be recourse to violence. To the contrary, if there was meaning in taking their own collective destiny in their hands once again, it was the obligation for both the individual and the group to examine and to settle the problems of public order, including that of thinking about the use of force, and to make rules and set limits for it. The prospect raised by the new conditions of setting up a national homeland was precisely that of testing fidelity to the above-mentioned Jewish ethics. During the exile it could only apply at the private level, but here it could finally be restored to the public domain. It was a difficult challenge, but what was really at stake, the rebirth of the Jewish nation, was found in finally having the opportunity to respond to that challenge.

Thus it is when one has the freedom to use force that the decision not to do so is really meaningful. Then the warning against the dangers of violence is addressed not only to harmless folk, as could be the case in exile, but rather to the Jewish people, as in the time of the prophets, so that they could correct their faults or, even better, avoid them. To protest against force in principle, when one has no means of using it, is too easy morally, since it demands nothing of the person asserting the principle.

It was in breaking with this Jewish condition of standing outside politics that the return to Zion was a healthy test. Whatever else it was, for "cultural", "spiritual" and "ethical" Zionists, the journey towards rebirth needed to be "Jewish", that is specific, easily seen and identifiable with a long tradition, more moral than religious, which preceded it. It was not to be a slavish imitation of the warrior values of the Greek or Roman empire, of the West in general, but was to take into account that non-violence with which the Jews, voluntarily or by force, had reacted to what they had endured. The poet Avigdor Hameiri suggests that putting down another person, beyond being a crime, is a denial of the Jewish spirit. *Kill?* he conjectures:

"Sensitive child that I had been,
opening a window for a fly that was freezing,
helping an ant in its struggle,
I, take a life?
Wield a sword?
My God! my God!
What should I do with the Jew in me?"[6]

By reading the past entirely differently, Berdichevsky justifies the integration of the use of force into the new Jewish spirit. The "change of values" associated with him and his work belongs to this worship of vital forces, of health, virility and the sword. He refuses to take the path of the "harmless". He vehemently affirms that he is helping to reappropriate a source which was repressed in exile and replaced by a sacred dedication to studies. From Joshua's conquest of Canaan to Samson's towering strength and the cunning of David in striking down Goliath, the Bible is full of warrior heroes and exalts their virtues; there are plenty of reports of military prowess. The real meaning of the military metaphors, emasculated by two thousand years of rabbinic tradition, was now to be restored.[7] Here was an epic spirit and material which ought to inspire the rebirth of the nation, if it was to replace two millennia of passivity with creative energy eager for action. And even more than the Bible, the story of the Maccabees, and the Jewish revolt against the Romans as reported by Flavius Josephus, provided references to dress this new image in the revered stories of the past.

For this debate between Ahad Ha'am and Berdichevsky on the role of force in the new Zionist ethics, the historic opposition between the partisans of Bar-Kochba and those of Yohanan Ben-Zacchai in the 2nd century over against the Roman occupation also served as a reference. The first thought an active resistance essential, a major insurrection, to go all the way in manifesting Israel's determination to throw off the occupation, even though it was extremely audacious and a lost cause from the beginning; but it would be a battle for honour and show at least the heroism of which Israel was capable. The other side thought quite the opposite: they thought the resistance should be spiritual, and since the balance of power was unfavourable, the strategy should be to flee and to set up a rabbinical academy at Yavna to preserve Jewish wisdom in response to difficult times: "no one who observes the will of the Lord can be ruled by any other nation." There is no doubt that Bar-Kochba had much more appeal for the Zionists, and the investment in its appeal was mythical, through both poetry and scientific research. Contradicting the entire Jewish tradition, which had repressed the memory of Bar-Kochba, it took on in fact for the first time an importance and a value never seen before.[8]

For Jabotinsky, to take part in war, to prepare for defence, is a matter of historic and even moral vision. War would provide the opportunity to bring the Jewish nation alongside the other European nations which had more or less all taken up arms to gain their freedom. Therefore it was necessary, perhaps even desirable, for Jews to be prepared to spill their blood in defence of their fatherland. There was no dearth of examples: the American revolution, the struggles for independence in Italy, Poland and Ireland. From there it was not far to the thought that a nation needs its own epic, and that its most heroic hours are those lived on the field of battle. The moment of truth had struck; it was time to enter into History, instead of fleeing as in the past; this, for Jabotinsky, was the meaning of independence, which one brought near by firmly taking the course of activism. It was in combat that a people really showed that it wanted to be free.

The defensive ethos

While rejecting violence for violence' sake, one should not be an ideological pacifist either, but find the right balance between the two, a defensive ethos which set limits on the use of force. In 1936, this was the attitude of restraint *(havagla)* towards any Arab aggression, proclaimed by Ben-Gurion. Except in cases of legitimate defence, this attitude excluded any punitive excursion, any form of revenge against civilians, even though Arab guerrillas made no distinctions between military, political or civilian targets. Even if diplomatic concerns were predominant in the final decision, ethical factors were not absent. In any case they formed the base of this defensive ethos of the *yishuv*, which the historian Anita Shapira identified as the synthesis among humanist and internationalist commitments inherited from the socialist tradition, from the psychological needs of the Zionist rebellion against Jewish passivity, and the taking into account of an armed element in the power relationships.[9]

An all-out war among all concerned would have buried forever any possibility of an immediate reconciliation between Jews and Arabs, which had to remain, cost what it might, the limitation on Jewish politics. This was the viewpoint within which the idea of "purity of weapons" *(tohar ha neshek)* was conceived, the specific term forged to designate one of the cardinal principles of Zionist-Socialist defence doctrine. It signified that the use of arms was subject to strict rules and must be exclusively defensive; that it would be either pure, or defiled forever, according to its absolute respect for these criteria.

Defensive ethos and militarism

Even though it was officially maintained, this defensive ethos was not averse to considering a spirit of initiative, even going over to an offensive strategy, but while maintaining the veto on any violence against innocent people. During the war of independence, in order to regain control of the situation, the authorities gave the green light to attacks against Arab villages which had served as bases for combatants. Thus the defensive ethos which had been in place from the beginning was partially

outmoded, largely due to military confrontation taking the place of nego-
tiation. But it was especially the arrival of the first generation of *sabras*
— not in the political leadership, which was provided by the veterans of
the second *alyah*, but in the military commands — which did much to
determine the profound change in the dominant ethos. Less ideological
and more laconic than their parents' generation, which had enjoyed talking about action as much as taking it, the *sabras* were little inclined to
ramble on about the purposes of action. They were not concerned with
the primacy of political considerations; what was important was military combat, offensive actions. In other words, there was a tendency to
think of force as a more efficient, adequate and tangible way to solve
problems.

In this regard, the *Shoah* had been the counter-example which should
never be followed again. The use of force, justified as legitimate self-
defence, was both a question of survival and a moral duty. The tragedy
of destruction which had been experienced during the *Shoah* must be
opposed by the rebirth of a strike force and of action. This was the condition for the Jewish people to become a subject in History and not its
eternal victims.

Remembering violence

In the Jewish tradition, memory plays a pre-eminent role. The divine
injunction to Israel was to listen *(Shema Israel)* and even more, to
remember *(zakhor)*. Furthermore, it is notable that this obligation is
mutual: just as the human beings do, God promises to remember the
covenant made with Israel. God commands the Jewish people to remember the seventh day, to keep it holy and to distinguish it from the other
days in the week. The people are called upon to remember that they were
once slaves in Egypt, so that they will not rigorously oppress strangers
among them. The Passover feast, or *Pessach*, is the commemoration of
that act which caused the people to come up out of Egypt, after many
wanderings, and they are to tell the story as if they themselves had been
actors in it.

Finally, there is another call to remember the violence to which they
have been subjected. "Remember," it says, "what was done to you by
Amalek." Various meanings have been ascribed to this injunction. The
most simplistic consists in interpreting it as an explicit legitimation of
vengeance. When Amalek exercises his power to do evil, and his victims
are not in a position to counter it, the only outlet for anger is to record
his name and to keep it until, in more favourable times, the balance of
power is changed, allowing the victims to punish him mercilessly for
his deed.

But this is an extension of the proposition, because the call is not
simply a call to vengeance. The instinct to take revenge is sublimated in
a demand limited to the faculty of remembering. Furthermore, it is not
what he is which is important, but what he did. It is the violence which

is to be condemned, not the identity — as such — of the person who committed it. It is this second aspect of the command which brings up the problem of identification. Who is Amalek? He is the hereditary enemy, he who is metamorphosed over and over, pursuing the Jewish people with his wickedness. The ambivalence here is that having a generic name makes him available for every use. He can be Haman in the story of Esther, or Titus, and in more recent times Shmielnitsky, who instigated the pogrom of 1648, Petliura during the civil war that followed the October revolution, and finally Hitler. It is no surprise that for many Jews in Israel, and perhaps in the diaspora as well, he has been reincarnated today in the form of Yasser Arafat. Beyond the perniciousness of such a reincarnation in itself, such vigilance can degenerate into a fixed idea, an obsession. The call to remember can become, if one is not careful, an explicit calling to think of nothing but retaliation in one's politics, to conduct one punitive expedition after another.

The truth is that it is not so much the identification of Amalek which appears everywhere in the public discourse as the reference to the *Shoah*. This is what dominates, beyond all other analogies, whether we are legitimising or condemning its use. All the violence which we suffer is automatically referred back to the *Shoah*. Paradoxically the comparison is far from being used to relativize people's judgment of the terrorist acts which regularly strike at Israeli civilians. It is not the results or the methods of the attacks, but definitely their intent to which people pay attention in establishing a continuity between the destruction of the Jews by the Nazis and the suicide bombings. Some people even go so far as to say that these actions are a barbarity which even the Nazis didn't think of. Rather than seeing in them, as one hears in the Western press, an ultimate expression of despair, people see in this extreme method a new tenacity in pursuing destruction, because it only results in increasing the toll of victims and in spreading panic. This massive presence of the *Shoah* as defining category demonstrates the role of memory in the constitution of the Israeli nation in the first place, and in its reconstitution. The evolution is considerable; it goes together with a phenomenal explosion of memories, and a growing difficulty for institutions to obtain a relatively homogenous consensus.

The Israeli ethos was initially knowingly constructed as the antithesis of the forms and anomalies of the diaspora. This opposition was explicitly consecrated in the designation of a day of official remembrance of the *Shoah* and of *gvura*, or heroism, which was intended to give the nation at its birth a model for both positive and negative reference. Memory has become, no longer only a matter of increased obligation, as for example in "Remember that you were slaves in Egypt," but of ruling out attitudes which are thought to be too passive. The tie between the creation of Israel and the *Shoah* calls for intense reflection: beyond the close proximity in time of the two events, the connection is undeniable for the nations of the world who approved the partition plan, the relation between cause and effect is evident. Whether it had been responsible, complicit or indifferent, after such a catastrophe the world could no longer oppose the Zionist demand for a Jewish state.

In Israel this memory of the *Shoah* now has a long history. It has seen numerous changes and upheavals, sometimes contradictory. It poses a singular challenge: what should be remembered, and how? For a long time the principle prevailed of an official national and public commemoration for that which concerns the people as a whole, and private commemorations for that which concerns individuals. The relations between these two ways have been modified since; now there is room for victims to be recognised in their uniqueness. "Every person has a name" is what this initiative is now called, and it consists of speaking the names of those who disappeared instead of allowing their identities and uniqueness to be dissolved in a generic term.

In any case, the most lively and bitter dispute now turns on what are called, without paying too much attention, "the lessons of the *Shoah*". Israelis are divided and sometimes in violent opposition on what should be done and what not, but no one denies that the *Shoah* is the source of lessons to be learned. One can distinguish broadly those who say that the memory of the *Shoah* should make us always vigilant in watching for all the forces of anti-Semitism which are seeking to harm the Jews.

Those on the other side insist on the universal dimension of the *Shoah* and what it demands of everyone, Jew or non-Jew — on one's own ethical commitment. These proponents fear the excesses of a commemoration which would lead to Israel's being isolated even more from the rest of the world, which encourages it to be deaf to all other sufferings because they are not as great as the *Shoah*. It is pretty obvious that this debate is used to evaluate the Israeli-Arab conflict. Each side invokes the memory of the Shoah, on one side to exempt oneself from obligation, on the other to redouble it.

This remains a memory in which an enormous amount is at stake, but rather than try in vain to see its particular lessons as opposed to universal ones, it would be good to give thought to the uniqueness of the *Shoah*; this uniqueness, however, should not be allowed to be seen, from the inside or the outside, as a means of withdrawing and closing ourselves off from others.

Denis Charbit

NOTES

[1] Charles Péguy, *Le Mystère de la Charité de Jeanne-d'Arc*. Paris: Gallimard, 1972, 331.

[2] At the same time we should remain somewhat wary of over-simplistic distinctions, which are too quick to divide humanity into that fateful "us and them" which has done so much damage.

[3] See the interesting thesis of David Biale in *Power and Powerlessness in Jewish History*, New York: Schocken Books, 1986. He shows, contrary to the accepted idea, that the diaspora Jews had conceived a model of political presence in history which was less passive than that described in Zionist ideology of "negation of the diaspora".

[4] However, it was a long way from making strident declarations to carrying them out. The first man to think of creating a "people's militia" in Palestine, Yehiel Michal Halperin, had to yield to the absence of resources and the lack of realism of this goal.

[5] Israel Schohat, "The Yishuv Defence Programme" (1912) in Ben-Zion Dinour (ed.), *Sefer toldot ha haganah (Book of the History of Defence)*, vol. 1, part 1. Tel Aviv: Ha Sifria Hazionit & Maarakhot Press, 1954, 235-236.

[6] Havigdor Hameiri, "Kill?", translated from the Hebrew by Joseph Milbauer, in Pierre Haiat's fine collection *Anthologie de la poésie juive du monde entier depuis les temps bibliques jusqu'à nos jours*, Paris: Mazarine, 1985, 312.

[7] One of the most frequent examples of this hermeneutic metaphor is calling God "the Lord of hosts". The tradition made the "hosts" the heavenly bodies, the planets and stars over which God reigns.

[8] Yehoshafat Harkabi, *Vision, not Fantasy: Realism in International Relations* (in Hebrew). Tel Aviv: Domino Press, 1982, 145.

[9] On the history and significance of this defensive ethos, see the masterly work by Anita Shapira, *Land and Power. The Zionist Resort to Force*, 1881-1948. New York/Oxford: Oxford University Press, 1992.

IMPRIMERIE
LUSSAUD

L'impression et le façonnage
de cet ouvrage
ont été effectués
à l'Imprimerie LUSSAUD
85200 Fontenay-le-Comte

Dépôt légal 2ᵉ trimestre 2005
n° 3892
N° d'impression : 204 037